Earnestly Contend
For the Faith

EARNESTLY CONTEND
FOR THE FAITH

Written by Mary R. Miller

Rod and Staff Publishers, Inc.
P.O. Box 3, Hwy. 172
Crockett, Kentucky 41413
Telephone: (606) 522-4348

Copyright 2007
By Rod and Staff Publishers, Inc.
Crockett, Kentucky 41413

Printed in U.S.A.

ISBN 0-7399-2383-8
Catalog no. 2227

1   2   3   4   5   –   15   14   13   12   11   10   09   08   07

CONTENTS

1. Childhood and Youth 11
2. Following God's Direction 18
3. Shepherding the Flock 29
4. The Churches of the Norfolk District 38
5. A Stand for Truth 45
6. A Bishop Without a Church 56
7. Facing the Challenge 64
8. Keeping the Faith 76
9. The New Church 81
10. The Blessings of a True Fellowship 85
11. Contending for the Faith to the End 91
12. "He . . . Yet Speaketh" 98

Foreword

In every generation, God raises up men who make a difference. They are not supermen or flawless nor necessarily geniuses, but they are faithfully dedicated to truth. Because they fear God, they do not compromise truth for expediency. These men willingly suffer for righteousness' sake. They are humble, feeling unworthy and incapable of the roles to which God calls them; yet, by stepping out in faith and by God's grace, they make a difference.

Eli D. Kramer was such a man. Many loved and respected him, whereas others disliked and scorned him. I must confess that I was among the latter for a time in my life. But his faithful life and teaching convicted me until at last I repented at the foot of the cross. There, in a matter of minutes, everything changed.

My earliest recollection of Brother Kramer was when I was eleven or twelve years old. My family lived several miles from Brother Kramer's aging parents in Southeastern Virginia. When he visited his parents, Brother Kramer would preach at the Deep Creek Mennonite Church, where my family attended. In time he moved to Southeastern Virginia and became pastor of the Deep Creek congregation. In 1948, the Virginia Mennonite Conference ordained him bishop, in which office he faithfully served until his death in 1967.

Brother Kramer was a man of God. His deepest desire was to know the mind of Christ. In his compassion, he often grieved for those who were turning away from the faith they once embraced. His insights amazed me. He saw dangerous changes in life and practice coming into the churches that to him were a certain prelude to apostasy. He vigorously preached against these trends, calling everyone under his care to stand true to the Scriptures.

In the churches, a downward spiral of apostasy continued until the time came when Brother Kramer could no longer remain in the conference. He and other conference leaders of similar convictions finally concluded that the only way to save themselves, their families, and those in their realm of influence was to form new congregations honoring Biblical principles. Time has shown that their concerns were valid.

In this book, the author gives us glimpses into the life and times of Brother Kramer and into some of the events that help shape his convictions. Brother Kramer was not without faults, and he would not have wanted to be portrayed as perfect. He probably would have preferred that this book not be written. It is not the purpose of this book to exalt the man. Rather, its purpose is to glorify and exalt our Lord and Saviour and to demonstrate to yet another generation the importance of faithful obedience. May it ignite in youth a vision of what God can and will do with a life that is dedicated to His service, and may they arise to "earnestly contend for the faith" in their generation.

—Marion E. Miller

*"Beloved, when I gave all diligence
to write unto you of the common salvation,
it was needful for me to write unto you,
and exhort you
that ye should earnestly contend for the faith
which was once delivered unto the saints."
Jude 1:3*

1

CHILDHOOD AND YOUTH

Eli D. Kramer was born to Daniel J. and Mary Ann (Schlabach) Kramer on December 26, 1899. The Kramers, then living in Kansas, moved to Plain City, Ohio, when Eli was very young.

Eli grew up in an Amish home with his eight brothers and six sisters. As with most Old Order Amish families, farming was a way of life for the Kramers. As a young man, Eli often strolled across the fields, bringing in the cows for milking. He spent many happy hours exercising his strong muscles by putting up hay, shocking and husking corn, and doing many other farm jobs.

One lovely fall evening, Eli was out alone amid the beauties of nature. The autumn breezes tossed his thick, wavy hair and swirled the falling leaves about him, but Eli was oblivious to his surroundings. The formerly carefree youth now puckered his brow in deep thought as his usual lightheartedness gave way to more solemn, sobering thoughts.

A number of youth just older than he planned to join the church in the fall. Eli considered joining the group; yet he hesitated, wondering what church membership really was all about. *What is this deep, unsatisfied longing in my heart that will not be quieted?* he wondered. *Joining the church brings with it much responsibility and accountability. How can I be sure that God is calling me? What more do I need?* The longing in his heart was very unsettling after the years of security and rest he had enjoyed in his childhood. He had never spent much time reading his Bible, nor had he seriously considered his accountability to God. But now he was troubled. His sins condemned him. His efforts to live a holy life often met with failure, though he really wanted to be good.

He did not join the group of applicants for baptism that fall. *I will clean up my life first,* he decided, *and get rid of some bad habits. When I am a church member, I will be a good one.* However, Eli soon found that he could not get rid of those habits. He needed the Lord, and he needed the church.

The following year, when he was seventeen, Eli spoke to the elderly bishop about his troubled heart. "I'm a failure and I'm lost; I need help," he told the bishop.

"You need to join the church," the bishop said. "Another instruction class will be starting soon, and we can include you in that."

Childhood and Youth

After going through a period of instruction with a class of young people, Eli concluded that he was ready for church membership. He found some satisfaction in that decision. Still he felt an urge to search for deeper meaning in life. Eli then began to read his Bible in earnest and to pay attention to the sermons. He desired a better understanding of life and of God, since he had not found the formula for overcoming his sinful nature, which expressed itself in bad habits.

Church was a priority in the Kramer home. Their family strictly adhered to the standards upheld in the local congregation and faithfully attended its services.

Eli experienced the many joys associated with living in a large family where the parents loved and accepted every child alike. Peace and contentment filled his home during his growing years. They had family picnics and strolls through the woods or meadow to see a newly discovered bird nest or to help a new calf to its feet. The family together enjoyed the much hard work on their farm. The hard times as well as the pleasant times drew the family together in a loving bond.

In the winter of 1918, a highly contagious influenza raged through Madison County. Though it was risky, community people helped each other when whole families were sick.*

---

* *Britannica* places the first outbreak of the influenza epidemic in the United States in March of 1918, which became widespread by the winter of that year.

Earnestly Contend for the Faith

When the flu reached the Kramer home, many friends and neighbors were already afflicted, and many had died. One by one, the Kramers also contracted the flu until none of them were able to care for the sick. The children cried for water, and burning fevers brought delirium. They became weak and faint, and were unable to leave their beds. Cooking nourishing meals, housecleaning, and bringing in wood to keep the fires going became impossible tasks. Neighbors took responsibility for their chores.

When the situation became desperate, a sincere young lady, Mary Miller, offered her help, despite the risk to her own life. Some of Mary's family, out of fear for their own safety, discouraged her going, though they knew the need was great. However, Mary volunteered to stay with the Kramers until the siege was over, to avoid exposing her own family. God blessed her sacrifice. All of the Kramers recovered, and Mary completely escaped the dreaded plague. When the Kramer family had recovered enough to get along without help, Mary returned to her home a few miles away.

Eli had watched Mary's life, and he admired the quiet, cheerful, selfless way she put her heart into the wearisome task of comforting the sick, changing beds, preparing food, and quieting the children. He noted the many deeds of love and helpfulness she found time for each day. A bond of friendship began to grow between Eli and the young sister who had come as an angel of mercy into their home at this time of distress.

She is the most outstanding girl I have ever met, Eli often thought. Attracted to the young sister, he

Childhood and Youth

began pursuing a friendship.

Being an extremely bashful young man, a number of months passed before he asked for the privilege to visit her in her home. When the request came, Mary readily accepted. Her parents also welcomed and arranged for the visit. More visits followed.

The miles between the Miller and the Kramer homes were usually covered on foot. This was not a trial to Eli, with his eagerness to see Mary. Their parents agreed that they should not spend time together every week, as they were still quite young. They willingly submitted, waiting as patiently as possible for the next visit.

As time went on, more visits were granted. Eli now sometimes rode on horseback to see Mary, and on rare occasions he took the buggy to take Mary to a singing. However and whenever he came, Mary always met him with a radiant smile that sent a thrill of joy to his heart.

Together they talked and planned, discussing not only the home they hoped to have one day and other earthly interests, but also the deep spiritual struggles they both were having. In their ignorant hearts was a yearning for an understanding of God.

Several years passed before Eli had the courage to ask Mary to be his wife.

After Mary had promised to give him her hand and heart, more serious thoughts struggled in Eli's mind. He began to consider more seriously his standing with God. *Is there something lacking? I'm not at rest,* he thought. *I just cannot overcome my bad habits.*

I truly want a happy, Christian home. I want the best for my family. I want to be a godly father and leader in our home. Will I join Mary's church, or will she join mine? Or dare we consider another possibility, such as leaving the church where we were brought up to join another church? Is the Lord, indeed, leading in my life at all? Eli wanted it settled in his own mind before burdening Mary with the decisions of their future.

When Mary sensed that something was bothering him, she asked, "Is something troubling you?"

"Yes," he replied, "and it is easier to share my concerns with you than with anyone else." Together they sought to find their way, discussing various possibilities.

When Eli and Mary began occasionally attending other churches, Eli's parents were deeply concerned. "You must settle down and be content in the church of your fathers," his father admonished him. "We tried to bring you up right. Why can't you be satisfied and forget this constant seeking for something better?"

Knowing his parents' grief, Eli also grieved. He loved his parents, but the longing in his soul would not be quieted.

Noticing this restlessness in his young nephew, Uncle Joe, a deeply spiritual man, suggested to Eli that it would be good for him and Mary to attend several times at the Mennonite church where he attended. Eli was acquainted with Uncle Joe's family and was impressed with their Christian lives. He had been convinced that their young people were certainly more

Childhood and Youth

spiritual than the ones with whom he associated. "Come with your heart open to God," his uncle invited. "Do not come for freedom from rules and standards."

"No, that is not what I have in mind," Eli agreed. "The strict rules of our church do not bother me, but I am seeking for the inner peace and stability that I have appreciated in you. I would desire for Mary and me to find that peace and stability before we start raising a family. I do appreciate my parents and the way they have brought up a large family, but somehow something seems to be lacking."

"I understand," Uncle Joe agreed. "I went through the same struggles when I was young. And I have found the plain teachings of the Scriptures to meet that need in my heart. I would suggest that you come and see."

Eli and Mary discussed this concern together and decided to spend time praying before deciding.

"I do not like to do something that causes my parents so much concern," Eli told Mary. "And I am sure your parents will feel much the same. But we have to give our own account to God. In our church we have tried to obey the rules, though we have often failed; but we have not found a deep, soul-satisfying experience like Uncle Joe's family seems to have found. I feel that God is calling me, but I do not understand the call. Perhaps we could find spiritual help in the Mennonite church. By holding to our old traditions, we can prove to our parents that we are not looking for a more liberal standard."

2

FOLLOWING GOD'S DIRECTION

However, on November 16, 1922, Eli and Mary were married in Plain City, Ohio, in the Amish church. They were happy together, but the struggle to find soul satisfaction continued. They desired assurance that all was well in their relationship with God.

By 1925, there were four in the Kramer family. Raymond and LaVina added great joy to the Kramer home, but they also added a weight of responsibility. *We must bring these children to God.* Eli pondered his responsibility. Then he pondered his own lack of understanding in spiritual things, a heavy burden indeed that he could not look upon lightly.

The search for truth and light continued. The Kramers endeavored to be faithful to their church, but they increasingly sensed a lack. Something was missing. Their parents reasoned that if they would

Following God's Direction

stop attending other churches they would not feel so confused. They submitted but began reading their Bible together more often. They longed for someone to help them understand the deep spiritual truths they were finding there.

About this time Uncle Joe stopped by again. "How are things going?" he asked when Mary answered the door.

"Oh, real good," she replied.

"Where is Eli?" Uncle Joe asked next.

"He is working with the carpenter crew this winter, since the farm work is slow," she answered, wondering what had brought Uncle Joe this time of the afternoon.

"I just stopped by to tell you we are having revival meetings over at West Liberty, Ohio. I thought maybe you and Eli would enjoy attending some evenings."

"I will tell him about it," Mary responded. "I don't know what he will decide."

"I will stop by at seven o'clock just in case you do decide to go," he replied before hurrying away.

As soon as Eli was home from work, Mary began, "Uncle Joe was here."

"What did he want?" Eli questioned, sensing a bit of urgency in his wife's voice.

"He would like for us to go with him to the revival meetings over at West Liberty tonight."

"I believe I'll go," Eli decided right away. "Don't you want to get the children ready quickly and go along?"

"I would love to," Mary admitted, "but I had better

keep the little ones in tonight. Perhaps if you go again, I will plan to go along."

"I hate to leave you alone with the little ones this evening after being away all day, but I would really like to know what is going on over there. Those people seem so genuinely happy and satisfied with their Christian experience. And more than that, the Bible says, 'By their fruits ye shall know them.' Since I have worked with several of them, I am seeing what I desire for my own life."

Mary nodded. "You go. We will be fine. I'll put the children to bed early, and then maybe we can all go tomorrow evening if you should decide to go again."

Until this time, Eli knew little about victory over the sin that bound him. Hard as he had tried, he had not been able to break the tobacco habit. Unwholesome speech was another habit he had tried and failed to break. He had wanted to when he had joined the church. He had tried to do everything right, but it was not in his power. *Those people in Uncle Joe's church seem different. I need what they have,* he often told himself.

After a moment, Eli continued, "You know, Mary, that dream I had the other night really disturbed me. I cannot shake it off."

"About the fearful thunderstorm?" Mary asked.

"Yes. God is speaking to me. After that dream was repeated the second time, I just cannot get it out of my mind. It was horrible—terrifying. It seemed as bright as day until suddenly I saw that dark cloud, and everything was instantly as black as night. That

Following God's Direction

was terrifying enough, but far more so when the thunder began to roll, almost deafening me, and the balls of fire flamed across the ground." Eli remembered every detail vividly as he rehearsed it.

"I was simply terrified when I rolled under the corncrib, trying to escape the storm. It looked like everything was on fire. I thought the end of the world had come, and I was not ready to meet God. After the storm passed, there were sparks of fire everywhere I looked, and I tried desperately to stamp them all out to keep the whole world from burning. I believed they were the sins in my life that I must stamp out. Then I awoke with great relief. I determined to do something to make my salvation sure, but I didn't know what to do. I fell asleep and dreamed it all over again in every detail. I was just as horrified the second time, and it was again just as real." Great beads of perspiration stood on Eli's forehead when he finished relating the dream.

"Yes, I will go with Uncle Joe and see what I can learn. Maybe we can just keep it quiet so our parents won't need to worry."

When Uncle Joe arrived, Eli was ready to go. At this first evangelistic meeting that he ever attended, Eli was deeply convicted. A new and deeper understanding of salvation dawned on him as he opened his heart to the Lord. He turned to the Lord in true repentance. He was genuinely converted that night, and experienced a peace and a consciousness of God's presence such as he had never known before.

At home several hours later, Eli was eager to share

his experience with Mary. His Bible open, he clearly explained to her the wonderful plan of salvation. Mary too, when she understood, gave her heart to the Lord that night. For the first time, they clearly understood the new birth and accepted it by faith. His dear wife was Eli's first convert. His joy was full.

After experiencing the new birth and the witness of the Spirit in their hearts, their fervor to serve their Lord and Master grew. Together they continued to seek God's will for their lives and their home.

In the Mennonite church at West Liberty, Eli and Mary were spiritually awakened. Here the church introduced them to spiritual life unlike any they had ever seen. They still had, however, a deep respect for their parents and for the church where they had grown up. But their loyalty was now shifting to fellowship at West Liberty, where they first found their loyalty to God.

Brother S. E. Allgyer gave bishop oversight at the West Liberty church. Those who knew him remember him as a conservative man with a deep concern for the church. One thing in particular that he is remembered for was his often-repeated statement to youth, "Remember who you are."

Brother Allgyer's spiritual insight often amazed Eli. This faithful, elderly man became the Kramers' spiritual father. He did not urge them to change their church membership quickly. He was always available to answer questions and encourage them as they sought God's will. He did encourage them to respond as God revealed Himself to them.

Following God's Direction

Before the third child, Daniel, joined the Kramer family on November 14, 1926, Eli and Mary had become members of the Mennonite church at West Liberty. On December 2, 1928, Martha, their fourth child, was born, to the delight of parents and siblings.

Eli humbly pleaded with his parents and with Mary's, hoping they would understand their choices. Both families, however, remained strongly opposed to the changes Eli and Mary had made, though they could find no fault with their personal lives. They were happy to see the victory Eli now had in his life, yet they were not convinced that he could not have had victory in the church he grew up in. Eli acknowledged the same, and yet West Liberty was where he first came to grips with his sin and where he first understood salvation.

By God's grace, Eli had overcome vulgar speech and the tobacco habit. This brought great rejoicing to him and his wife. Their faith was strengthened as they recognized God's work in their hearts.

The joy the young Kramer family experienced in their conversion was evident. In his zeal for the salvation of others, Eli began to witness, even though he was often misunderstood and rebuked for his earnestness. Many of his family and friends took his concerns to be a holier-than-thou attitude and were not willing to listen.

However, others in the Plain City area, after seeing the spiritual life of this zealous young couple, also became interested in the Mennonite church. Sincere young seekers often came to Eli for help. Again, he was criticized harshly for trying to draw others with him out of the church where they had been raised.

Eli had no desire to be a troublemaker, but remembering his own years of distress and uncertainty, his compassion constrained him to help every soul he could. The concerns of his family and friends were a burden to Eli, but he never refused to share the good news of salvation with them.

Brother Allgyer gave guidance to the growing interest in the Plain City area. A small, unused schoolhouse was located, which was available for rent. He inquired to see if there was enough interest to have services there to save the travel distance to West Liberty, since most of the seekers in that area traveled by horse and buggy. Brother Allgyer found an overwhelming amount of interest, so the building was rented for services.

To begin with, Brother Allgyer or one of his fellow ministers was there to preach or have a Bible study several times a month. They also had weekly Sunday school.

The small group grew as more souls were converted. After some time, Brother Allgyer suggested organizing a church and ordaining one from among them. Counsel from the group showed that they welcomed the idea, so they began praying and planning.

The small congregation then started a weekly prayer service. These were very solemn occasions. The need for a resident minister was discussed in these meetings. They unitedly and earnestly sought God's direction in this important matter.

Following God's Direction

Brother Allgyer then set the dates for the nomination and ordination services. The church nominated the brethren Abraham Kauffman and Eli Kramer.

Brother Allgyer interviewed the two brethren nominated by the brotherhood. Both brethren met the qualifications and were willing to serve as minister if God called. Both considered seriously the responsibility they would have, if chosen. Both committed themselves to work together to build the church if the other were chosen.

On a Sunday morning at the ordination service, the lot was used to discern God's choice. Through this process, God chose Brother Abraham Kauffman to serve as minister.

The church prospered spiritually and grew in numbers. The members and minister worked together harmoniously. They soon built a new building to accommodate the growing interest.

In 1933, the church sensed the need for additional leadership for the growing congregation. Again, Brother Allgyer proposed an ordination from their group. The counsel of the church was favorable for a deacon ordination.

The ordination service was on December 3, 1933. Again, Brother Eli Kramer was one of the nominees, sharing the lot with several other brethren.

After the message at the ordination service, the time came for the Lord to choose by lot one from among the nominees. All present waited prayerfully and expectantly as each brother rose from his seat, walked to the table in front of the auditorium, and chose a book. In one of those books was the slip of paper that would show whom God had chosen. No one but God knew which book contained the lot.

After the nominees were again seated, each with his book, Brother Allgyer stepped over to the row of brethren. One by one, he took the book out of their hands and carefully looked for the lot. From Eli's book he drew the slip of paper and read distinctly, " 'The lot is cast into the lap; but the whole disposing thereof is of the LORD.' "

With bowed head, Eli humbly accepted his charge as the hands of the bishop were laid on his head. The elderly bishop spoke words of counsel and encouragement to Brother Kramer before leaving that evening. "Earnestly contend for the faith," he admonished.

When they arrived home from the ordination service, Eli placed his five-year-old daughter, Martha, on the heater to help her get warm. From her perch she looked up at her father and asked, "Are you a preacher now?"

Brother Kramer took his calling seriously, and with this additional responsibility, he and Mary found their schedule crowded. Counseling, visiting the sick, and admonishing erring members occupied much of their time. However, a day was never too full to take time for every seeking soul who found the way to their door. Everyone found a warm welcome in their home, and left encouraged. Many unfaithful ones, sensing Eli's deep concern for their souls, were brought to repentance. Many seeking souls found spiritual enlightenment in the humble Kramer home.

Eli often felt hard-pressed for time for all his God-given responsibilities, yet he found God faithful in supplying each need. Together the family planned and worked hard, sharing many happy experiences as God rewarded their faith in Him through the years of financial struggles.

Soon after Eli's ordination, an elderly Amish bishop contacted him. The bishop had tried for a long time—by his own efforts—to live a faithful life. He felt frustrated with his inability to live up to what he knew to be God's standard of holiness.

By God's grace and wisdom, young Brother Kramer led the older brother to a new birth experience. Experiences of leading souls to Christ were numerous and a great source of rejoicing to Eli.

At one point, the emotional show of religious fervor of some Pentecostal neighbors attracted Eli. In his inexperience, he became quite interested. Brother Allgyer's watchful eye prevented disaster. He encouraged the younger brother to observe the lives of those people carefully, comparing what he saw with the Scriptures. He did not dampen Eli's zeal, but directed it into right channels. "We can use that kind of zeal in the Mennonite church to promote true spirituality," he challenged. "But don't let impressive testimonies become confused with true holiness."

Brother Kramer took to heart the older brother's counsel and searched the Scriptures. As he also carefully observed his neighbors' lives, it did not take him long to understand where his leanings would take him. He often thanked God that he was spared being influenced away from the truth. This experience taught him to be very cautious with any teaching that emphasized emotional experience without holiness of life.

3

SHEPHERDING THE FLOCK

In 1936 the young church at Plain City, Ohio, received a call from the Ohio Conference, asking for ministerial help for a mission outreach in Meadville, Pennsylvania. Brother Allgyer spoke of the need to the Kramers.

"Would you be willing to respond to this need?" he inquired.

The Kramers talked it over, prayed about it, and soon returned their answer. "Yes, we are willing to take this as a call from the Lord, if the congregation releases us."

The need for a minister in Meadville was brought before the congregation. The Meadville congregation had no minister, and the Plain City church had both Abraham Kauffman and Eli Kramer. After seeking the Lord's will, the church consented to release their deacon, though they regretted to see him leave.

The Kramer family soon moved. It was in the Meadville setting that the four Kramer children grew up.

After working a short time with the church in Pennsylvania, Brother Kramer realized that some of his members had worldly involvements. He worked at ridding the church of the things that were detrimental to the spiritual life of the congregation, but he soon realized that the Ohio Conference did not share his convictions on many issues. This lack of support from the conference hindered his work, but it did not change Brother Kramer's loyalty to the truth.

Then the real test came. Jobs were hard to find in the area during the Depression years. Brother Kramer had sensed the Lord's blessing in locating a job in a nearby town. Several months after Brother Kramer began this job, the boss called him into the office one morning.

"Kramer," the boss began, "the labor union is in here, as you know."

Eli nodded. "Yes, I know." This was not the first time it had come up. He had firmly stated his convictions on other occasions, and the subject was dropped, but this time the boss seemed agitated. Eli realized he was facing a crisis. In the few moments that the boss paused, several things raced through Eli's mind.

Times are hard. The mission board is not able to send us sufficient funds. How can I afford to lose my job? But can I afford to compromise convictions based

Shepherding the Flock

on the Word of God? No! I can never do that. Though he did not know what the future held, Eli was thoroughly convinced that he could not compromise. If it meant losing his job to follow the Lord, the Lord would bless the loss.

"Well, it is final this time," the boss continued. "You have no alternative. You either join the union, or—"

"I cannot do that," Eli stated firmly.

"Plenty of men are waiting for a job, you know." The boss looked steadily at him.

"Yes, I know. It won't be a problem for you to fill this position."

"We hate to lose you. Your work is excellent, and you've been dependable," the boss continued. He paused again. "Couldn't you reconsider? Isn't there some way? You could sign up as a member and take no active part. I don't see how that could hurt you."

When Eli did not budge from his position, the boss continued, "We need you. You won't be able to get a better job anywhere. We live in hard times."

"Yes," Eli agreed, "I know all that, but I cannot violate my conscience. The Bible teaching is clear. I cannot be a member of the union. I've explained that to you before."

"Yes." The boss nodded impatiently. He handed Eli a check and dismissed him.

Brother Kramer walked out of the office, his needs weighing heavily on his mind. What now?

Already the mission board had not been able to send sufficient funds to pay the bills for the most meager living for his family and for the needs of the new mission church. How would he keep gas in his car, or even keep the old thing running? And what about family responsibilities?

Brother Kramer committed the situation to the Lord, knowing that he had done what was right. He was at rest. He had not made this decision rashly. He had considered it thoroughly and acted according to what he believed the Scriptures taught. He would not be involved in an unequal yoke with unbelievers. He would make any sacrifice rather than violate Scriptural principles.

Mary was concerned about the loss of his job, but she stood with her husband in his decision. They would stand together for truth in any circumstance.

Soon it was rumored through the community that the new minister had lost his job. Some of the members in the congregation were concerned. Some were indifferent. A few were critical: "You have to belong to the union. There is no way out these days."

"No," Brother Kramer told them calmly, "we would rather obey God and experience whatever hardships He allows than to compromise. The Lord will provide."

"He will help those who help themselves," one member commented.

The Kramers were grieved with these attitudes. Brother Kramer had hoped that his stand would be a testimony that would help his members to understand the need to clear the church of harmful involvements with the world. In spite of criticism, he remained firm in his stand.

Shepherding the Flock

Some said that he had begun to take an ultraconservative position on issues, but no one could support that by fact. Many godly people held the same views on these issues that Eli did. Why? It was because they lived by the same Book.

A fellow Mennonite employed at the same factory where Brother Kramer had worked joined the labor union to keep his job and because of the promise of a good retirement pension. He felt that he had to have both because of his family.

In his old age, this man lamented his course in life. The pension ended up being an empty promise. He died a man without a pension because no funds were available. Sadder yet, his family was lost to the world.

Day after day Eli looked for work. The situation was getting desperate, but his faith in God was strong. God had never failed him. With serenity, he faced each new day. With the same confident trust in God, he fulfilled his ministerial duties, teaching his people the importance of obedience to God's Word by both precept and example, regardless of the circumstances.

After months of skimping to make ends meet, the time came when Eli and Mary did not know where their next meal would come from. With deep concern, the young father gathered his family around him one morning. "Children," he began, "you know we have no money, and our food is all gone. We are going to pray together and ask God to provide for us in whatever way He sees best. Then we will be content with what He supplies." He smiled lovingly at the children, eagerly looking to their father to meet their needs.

With deep awe for their father and his God in their hearts, the children knelt before God with their parents. They were confident of His loving care.*

"Kind Father in heaven," Eli prayed earnestly, "You have so abundantly provided for all our needs. We come to You again, asking You to supply our need for food. Whether You supply work or provide some other way, we commit that to You, knowing that in Your wisdom You will do what is best. We ask that You would provide what we need to strengthen us for the work You have for us to do. We thank You, for we know Your way is best."

Following his prayer, Mary led out, and then each of the children, asking God to meet their needs by supplying daily bread.

As he was leaving for another day of job hunting, his youngest daughter came to him and said, "God will send us food; we prayed that He would."

All day Eli walked the streets. Nothing! In despair, he turned homeward. No job, no money, no food. Near the end of that day, Eddie Knight, a member of the mission church, stopped in. Eddie was a milkman, and he occasionally brought milk to the Kramers. But today he brought a head of cabbage and gave it to Brother Kramer, explaining that it must have fallen from a passing produce truck. God did send food!

---

* Daughter Martha: "I can well remember the faith our parents had and how our needs were supplied."

Shepherding the Flock

Eli entered the house. "Mother," he called, "come see what I have."

Without being called, four eager children followed their mother to the kitchen. "Father, what is it?" several children asked at once.

"The biggest head of cabbage I've ever seen," their father said triumphantly, his eyes twinkling as each child reached to touch the large green leaves.

"Cabbage!" Mother exclaimed in surprise.

"Yes!" Eli chuckled. "We didn't specify what we wanted, and the Lord sent cabbage."

"Where did it come from?" one of the children asked.

"I suppose it fell off one of those large produce trucks, and a brother from the mission gave it to us. Let's kneel and thank the Lord for sending us food," Eli suggested. The whole family knelt there in the kitchen and thanked God with true gratitude in their hearts.

That night the Kramers had cabbage wedges sprinkled with salt for supper. How good the cabbage tasted to everyone.

About this time, the mission board asked Brother Kramer to move out into the country with his family, so that he could raise some food and perhaps obtain work. Eli found work on a farm, where the boys could also help with the work, but it was nine miles from the church. The old car gave out completely, so he often walked to church and left the family behind.

Many times Eli started out with his Bible under his arm, only to be picked up by strangers who offered him a ride. Their testimony was that they were not afraid to pick him up when they saw his Bible.

The summer supply of food did not always last through the long, hard winters. One winter a neighbor brought a bushel of potatoes, some the size of a quarter, some smaller. "I thought you could feed these to your pigs," he offered. "We have more than we need, and I thought these might at least help fatten your pigs while feed is scarce."

The pigs never got any of those potatoes. Mary was happy enough to scrub those potatoes and serve them with the peelings to the family. As she prepared potatoes, Mary sang, " 'God is still on the throne.' "

Eli found work—thus the Lord supplied their needs. He also continued to work with the Meadville church for a number of years, but there were still some involvements with the unequal yoke. After talking this over with the bishop in charge, Brother Kramer was disappointed to find that the conference body would not stand behind him in requiring a clear break from these involvements.

After some years, Eli and Mary began to consider relocating. They sought the Lord's will and then waited on Him.

Eli's parents now lived about two miles from the Deep Creek Mennonite Church, a Virginia Conference church, near Deep Creek, Virginia. The elder Kramers were members of the Old Order Amish church in the area. When Brother Kramer went to the Norfolk area of Virginia to visit his aging parents, he preached at Deep Creek.

Shepherding the Flock

Early in the 1940s, Brother Kramer met Virginia Conference brethren who believed him to be right in his convictions. From this contact, they asked Brother Eli for a series of revival meetings in the Deep Creek church, then a small congregation in southeastern Virginia without a local minister.

Brother Kramer was impressed with the response there. His heart was drawn to these people who seemed to be sincerely seeking to serve the Lord.

In mid-July, 1945, Brother Kramer received an invitation from two ministers of the Norfolk District, Clayton Bergey and Amos D. Wenger, Jr., to move to Deep Creek to serve the congregation there as pastor.

Again the Kramers prayerfully considered the call, submitting themselves to God's will. The Ohio Conference released Brother Kramer, and moving plans began. A July 28 diary entry reads, "I am persuaded to go on the best divine imparted understanding."

The Lord led, opening the way for Eli and Mary, with their youngest child, Martha, to move to Deep Creek in Virginia in 1945. The second to youngest, Daniel, joined them later.

By this time, Raymond, the oldest son of the Kramers, was married. After his release from Civilian Public Service (CPS), he was ordained to the ministry on November 17, 1946, and became the pastor of the Meadville church.

4

THE CHURCHES OF THE NORFOLK DISTRICT

Mt. Pleasant Church

The first Mennonite family had come to Norfolk County in southeastern Virginia in the year of 1895 and had settled in the Mt. Pleasant community. These Mennonites came seeking inexpensive farmland. Land prices had become depressed due to the freeing of slaves thirty years earlier, which in turn disrupted the plantation economy of the rural south.

A few other Mennonites began to arrive by the year 1900, and by the close of 1910, there were twenty-two families at Mt. Pleasant. An early leader in the congregation was J. D. Wert, ordained as pastor in 1905 and in 1908 as bishop of the Fentress (Mt. Pleasant) and the Warwick Districts of the Virginia Conference.

The minister and evangelist A. D. Wenger, Sr., arrived in 1908 and ably served the church until 1922, when he was called to serve as president of Eastern Mennonite School. T. J. Wenger arrived in 1908 and was active as deacon for many years. Isaac Eby, also a deacon, arrived in 1908. Another deacon, Clayton Bergey, came in 1910 and served as deacon until he became pastor in 1922.

In 1912, J. D. Wert was relieved of his official responsibilities and later excommunicated because of moral failure. George R. Brunk, Sr., was then given bishop oversight of the Mt. Pleasant congregation. Brother Brunk served in this capacity until shortly before his death in 1938.

In 1937 Amos D. Wenger, Jr., was ordained to the ministry and served as pastor for many years. Roy Wenger was ordained deacon in 1936, as was Abram Wenger in 1954.

Deep Creek Church

The first Mennonite family moved into the Deep Creek area of Norfolk County, Virginia, in 1933. Because of personal health problems and stress in his Ohio church, a bishop, Joseph Mast, with his family moved from the Martin's Creek area of Holmes County, Ohio, to Warwick County, Virginia, approximately forty-five miles to the west of the Deep Creek community. In 1933 he moved his family to Deep Creek.

The Asa Hertzler, the Mark Hertzler (Asa's brother), the Earl Yoder, and the Emanuel Troyer families were the next Mennonite families arriving in 1934. Soon the Monroe Miller, Paul Zook, Henry Shelly, Fred Miller, Joe Slabaugh families, and others joined the first families. In 1937, the church built a meetinghouse on West Road, which is still in use by a Virginia Conference church today.

Joseph Mast served as the first pastor of the fledgling congregation until his death in 1938 at the age of sixty-three. He did not serve as bishop. The Virginia Conference supplied bishop oversight.

From the time of Brother Mast's death until the arrival of the deacon Eli Kramer seven years later, the ministry of the Mt. Pleasant congregation, twelve miles east of Deep Creek, supplied ministerial help.*

In 1945 the Kramers moved into the Deep Creek area. Their new home, the former home of Eli's parents, was a large, white-frame house in the middle of the small farming community. About a dozen church families lived in the area around them.

The congregation at Deep Creek welcomed the Kramers. The Kramer's youngest daughter, Martha, was soon teaching in the Christian day school at Deep Creek. Within a year of their arrival, the church gave Brother Kramer a charge as minister of the congregation. The congregation rejoiced greatly to have a local minister at last, after about seven years of depending on the Mt. Pleasant ministry to serve their congregation. During those years, Amos Wenger or

---

* The history of the churches taken from the book *Building at Mt. Pleasant,* by Robert W. Mast.

The Churches of the Norfolk District

Clayton Bergey had been there twice a month for preaching services. The evening services, the in-between Sunday mornings, the Sunday schools, and the Bible studies were conducted by the local brethren.

The church appreciated Brother Kramer's ministry in those first years. His message was one of cross bearing and self-denial. He seemed to sense that some liked his preaching until the cross came into focus. Events in the following years proved this to be true. One of the ministers from the Mt. Pleasant congregation suggested that perhaps Brother Kramer should take regular turns preaching there as well. "The people have taken a liking to your preaching," he said.

Brother Kramer replied, "That will change."

Brother Kramer was always alert to dangers that might threaten his home, and this sometimes brought accusations of being critical. At one point, his daughter began a friendship with a young man among her associates. To the watchful father, it was soon evident that the young man did not evidence a spiritual mind. The young man's interest in his daughter caused him concern. He asked his daughter to immediately break the friendship.

Some years later his daughter expressed appreciation for her parents' loving advice, though at the time it hurt. In her confidence and love for her parents, she had responded to their wishes. Later she married with the approval of her godly parents and enjoyed the benefits of their foresight.

The Kramers were a close-knit family. One of Brother Kramer's children said that the happiest memories of her childhood were the times her family spent together in family worship, singing and praying together and discussing the Scriptures.

Since there was no other ordained brother in the local congregation, Brother Kramer also filled the place of deacon. In 1946 he felt the need for additional ministerial help. The bishops' goal was to have a plural ministry for each congregation. Choosing from within the congregation was considered the Scriptural pattern.

Many of the more serious-minded brethren spent much time in prayer in preparation for this work. Brother Harvey Mast was ordained deacon in the fall of 1946. On October 8, 1948, in another ordination, Brother Harvey was ordained minister, and he worked harmoniously with Brother Kramer for many years. Brother Charles Warfel was ordained to fill the role of deacon in late August of 1949.

The Deep Creek congregation worked closely with the Mt. Pleasant congregation, who had earlier provided ministers for the Deep Creek pulpit. Neither congregation had a local bishop. Brother S. H. Rhodes and Brother J. R. Driver, from Waynesboro, Virginia, had bishop oversight of the two Norfolk district congregations until 1948, three years after the Kramers' arrival in Virginia.

In 1948 the churches of the Norfolk district called for a bishop ordination. After much prayer and seeking God's will, the nonresident bishops along with the

The Churches of the Norfolk District

congregations decided to go ahead with that work. The new bishop would be chosen from among the ministers. Amos Wenger and Eli Kramer both had the required number of nominations for ordination, so they used the lot. Brother Kramer drew the lot. He would relieve the Harrisonburg bishops of much travel to care for these churches in southeastern Virginia.

In the late 1940s and early 1950s, mission interests developed in the Norview community, located about eighteen miles northeast of the Deep Creek community and about nineteen miles northwest of the Mt. Pleasant community. In his zeal for the outreach work of the church, Brother Kramer was soon involved in the small mission at Norview. He conducted home visitation and cottage meetings for several years, after which a meetinghouse was built on what is now 915 Widgeon Road, Norfolk, Virginia.

Brother Eli continued his work at Norview until 1951, when Brother Levi Kramer was ordained for this work on December 2, 1951. Brother Levi served as pastor until 1956, when he and his family moved to Amelia, Virginia. Brother Paul Landis served as pastor from 1956 until he and his family moved to Hartville, Ohio, in July of 1959.

During their first days in Virginia, the Kramer's opened their home to Eli's widowed mother. She spent her days rocking contentedly in front of the large living room window, her hands busy with sewing or with weaving grass mats. Her stories of years past were a delight to a number of young sisters in the church who would occasionally spend an evening with her to free Brother and Sister Kramer for church work. These experiences gave them insight into Brother and Sister Kramer's homelife. Grandmother Kramer's presence graced their home for two years until she went to live with her daughter, the Mahlon Weaver family.

In 1953 she moved in with her son, Levi Kramer, until the Lord called her home on October 29, 1955, at 79 years of age.

5

A STAND FOR TRUTH

On June 6, 1948, Brother Eli Kramer had been given the bishop's charge, and so he became resident bishop of the Norfolk district of the Virginia Conference. The Mt. Pleasant congregation near Fentress and the Deep Creek congregation near Deep Creek were the only two churches in the district at that time.

Brother Kramer had already proven his faithfulness in church administration. He dealt with each situation in the fear of God. He was not a harsh man, but he was firm on truth. Being a tenderhearted, compassionate man, he was deeply grieved when a member suffered or was in spiritual danger. His spiritual concern and naturally cheerful disposition endeared him to many of those whom he served.

He now felt the weight of his new responsibility and continued to lead with zeal in an effort to rid the churches of inconsistencies. He filled his place faithfully, teaching, admonishing, warning, and encouraging. Although he contended for truth and holy living, he was not contentious. This faithful leader was not fooled by lip profession when the evidence of a holy life was absent. He preached vigorously and though slow to discipline, when warning and exhortation failed, he disciplined with loving compassion.

During and following World War II, there was a tremendous population growth in the Norfolk–Virginia Beach area of Virginia. This was due to the buildup of a massive military complex in southeastern Virginia, which began in the 1930s and brought booming business and high-income jobs to the area.

The Deep Creek congregation also grew rapidly. The question came up whether to enlarge the building or start an outreach. Harvey Mast, minister, with his family and several other families felt a burden to move away from the Norfolk area. The Nike missile base—which had taken part of the Mast farm—was now located only about 1,000 feet from their house.

The congregation at Deep Creek was very reluctant to release Brother Mast. However, Brother Kramer, Brother Mast, and the other conference bishops felt that it would be a wise move, be good for the church, and would provide a witness in a new community. The two churches would still work together, with Brother Kramer taking the responsibility of bishop oversight in the new congregation at Amelia, Virginia.

The church granted a release to Brother Harvey

for the work at Amelia. Brother and Sister Mast with their twelve children were greatly missed at Deep Creek after they moved. Brother Harvey's aged mother, Sister Mary Mast, also moved with them to Amelia, which was located about thirty-five miles west of Richmond, Virginia, or about one hundred thirty-five miles west of the Norfolk area. This move took place in March of 1955.

Several months later, minister Leroy Hooley and his family joined the Masts. The Pilgrim congregation in Amelia County, Virginia, was organized yet that year. Most of the families that moved to Amelia in those early years were from the Deep Creek congregation, including the Jonas Mast, Harvey Mast, John J. Miller, Oliver Weaver, Vernon Weaver, and Roman Miller families, as well as others. The worldly trends that were developing in the Norfolk district no doubt had much to do with this development and influenced not a few to make the move to Amelia.

But the Deep Creek congregation and the Pilgrim congregation at Amelia enjoyed a good working relationship. Harvey Mast and Leroy Hooley were the first leaders at Amelia and received full support for the outreach from Brother Kramer, who served as their bishop. The new congregation, however, did not enter the church councils of the Norfolk district.

As the years passed, Brother Kramer saw that the ministry in the Norfolk district was not united in their thinking about the apostasy in the churches. He took issue with a number of unscriptural practices and worldly trends that had come into the churches, such as membership in labor unions and milk co-ops, the wearing of jewelry and ties, women cutting their hair, employment in public works on Sunday, and other things. But without the full support of his fellow ministry, it became a losing battle, especially at Mt. Pleasant.

Brother Kramer pled that it was time to take a stand on these issues. He contended that if the dollar were out of the picture, it would not be hard to see what was right or wrong in relation to the unequal yoke. His pleas to the ministry and the people went largely unheeded, until finally in 1957, he decided that he would not serve Communion to the Mt. Pleasant congregation.

The Mt. Pleasant congregation did not commune for about two years as Eli tried in vain to unite the ministry and call the people to repentance. In time, he appealed for help to the Executive Committee of the Virginia Conference.

The Executive Committee then appointed bishops Daniel W. Lehman and John L. Stauffer of Harrisonburg, Virginia, to work with Brother Kramer.[1]

The committee was provided to oversee this situation but was not intended to supplant Brother Kramer nor to restrict him in his activities. However, in the spring of 1959, Lehman and Stauffer came to Mt. Pleasant and led in counsel meeting and Communion services without further notice to Brother Kramer. And in

---

[1] Reports from D. W. Lehman and J. L. Stauffer to the Executive Committee on Nov. 27, 1959, confirm this appointment.

July of the same year, Philip Miller was ordained to the ministry at Mt. Pleasant without Brother Kramer's counsel or involvement.

The Executive Committee's involvement up to this time was only with the Mt. Pleasant congregation and not with the other churches in the district. Brother Kramer was still active in the oversight of the Deep Creek and Norview congregations in the district, as well as in the Amelia congregation, and generally had good support from these churches.

In the Deep Creek congregation, however, Brother Kramer still saw a number of long-standing inconsistencies. He was grieved, and with prayers and tears pled for a deeper commitment to God.

In the early years most of the members attended services regularly on Sunday mornings, but they attended poorly at the Sunday evening and the midweek prayer services.

Some were unwilling to live up to the written standard. Brother Kramer was deeply burdened as he realized that though the written standard called for one thing, what others generally expected of the members of the conference was quite different. On many points, the written standard was embraced as an ideal only. The young people dressed in plain, modest attire on Sunday, as their parents did, but their appearance in town or at a social gathering was far different. Apparently, neither the church nor the parents had taken issue with the problem, and Brother Kramer became increasingly aware of the spiritual indifference and drift that was taking its toll on the churches. This was especially true of the Mt. Pleasant congregation, though there was much reason for concern at Deep Creek as well.

Many young sisters had taken jobs in worldly homes or in hospitals. Many young men were employed in public works. So Brother Kramer began teaching on the need for a life of simplicity and the dangers of materialism.

Many activities, including literary societies and other social gatherings, involved youth from Mt. Pleasant as well as Deep Creek. There were even the occasional attendances at the theaters. Older members had frowned upon this, but when Brother Kramer became aware of the disorder, he insisted on discipline to curb these worldly practices. Many families responded well, making changes for the good, but not all.

The Kramers spent many evenings visiting in the homes of the members or having members in their home. For a time, weekly singings in the Kramer home encouraged as many as attended. They worked and prayed with those who came within their doors and won their confidence and respect.

Often when the Kramers traveled to another state for conference meetings or other special meetings, they took several young people with them. These were excellent opportunities to become closer to the youth and learn of their struggles and aspirations. Those trips are treasured memories to many who grew up in the Deep Creek community in the '40s and '50s. During conference sessions, these youth sat where they could watch Brother

Kramer's face. This was especially true after they noticed that he was often opposed for standing firm on some Biblical principle.

"Sometimes I am hardly sure what is sound, Scriptural reasoning when the ministers differ," one sister said. "But if I watch Brother Kramer's expression, I can catch whether he is pleased or displeased with the conclusions. That helps me."

In the last few conference sessions that Brother Kramer attended, he spoke out courageously against the wrong trends in the church. But the liberal ministers calling for tolerance often squelched his concerns.

When the life insurance question came up, Brother Kramer spoke against this compromise. "I am concerned that we will lose our trust in God," he said. "We will look to insurance to meet our needs instead of helping each other."

He met strong opposition. "We are living in a different age and must adapt to our culture," they reasoned.

"The world is changing," Brother Kramer agreed, "and getting farther from God all the time, so there must be an ever-widening gap between us and the world. The church must remain the same—not just a few years behind the world—or we will finally end up in the world."

"But we are in the world," one brother persisted in all sincerity. "We must relate to present-day trends. We've got to live!"

"No!" Brother Kramer responded. "We can die." Then he added with fervor, "But we've got to remain true to God if we expect to live eternally."

The Kramers went home disappointed from the conference meeting.

Brother Kramer had preached and taught, hoping to see an immediate response as he had seen several years earlier. When this was not the case, he realized that it was his responsibility before God to take positive action. Things could not continue as they were.

Members were contacted personally and warned that the church would take action unless they responded to sound Bible teaching.

Brother Kramer then heard from the bishops of the Executive Committee. "You may not take action against members without our consent" was the message as Brother Kramer understood it. It was further his understanding that the Committee considered silencing him.[2]

Brother Kramer was shocked! *How am I to fulfill my God-given responsibility in the church? Someday I will give account to God. I must obey God. I am only trying to carry out my responsibility according to the Word.*

Surely the conference body, under which he was working, meant for him to keep a pure church, exercising whatever discipline was needful to do so. He

---

[2] Those who knew Eli confirm that he had these impressions, but the letters from the Executive Committee do not indicate either. However, a Committee member had asked Eli if he knew what the Committee was planning to do. He did not. They were planning to silence him, the Committee member said.

carefully and respectfully explained the conditions to them, trusting that there had surely been some misunderstanding. But no, he had understood correctly. The Executive Committee did express concern for worldliness, but little was done to correct the problem. One of the bishops observed that the Norfolk district was in better shape than most of the other districts in the conference as far as worldliness was concerned.

It should be noted, however, that events in the Virginia Conference in the next few years proved that in spite of expressed concern, little was done or perhaps could have been done, to stop the worldward movement.

Brother Kramer was grieved by the lack of support from the Executive Committee. He had accepted his charge as from God. Now in the fear of God, he and his faithful ministry had to administer their duties as those who would give an account to Him. But how could it be done without apparent rebellion against the larger conference body?

Brother and Sister Kramer rejoiced to see changes as evidence of growing conviction in the Deep Creek congregation. Dresses were lengthened, many bright, flashy colors were put away, fashionable hairdos were changed, and a more-appropriate covering size was being adopted. Brother Kramer was seeing some results of his labors. However, dare he ignore the members who were not responding? Would not a little leaven eventually leaven the whole lump?

He faced even more resistance from the Mt. Pleasant congregation. They preferred to work with the two bishops appointed by the Executive Committee.

Brother Harvey Mast with the Pilgrim congregation in Amelia, Virginia, continued to stand with Brother Kramer in his convictions and constantly encouraged him to remain firm. Many in the Deep Creek congregation stood with him as well.

Brother Kramer continued to administer the way he believed to be Scriptural, regardless of the opposition he faced. This included dealing with known sin in the lives of members in his charge. He did not succumb to the ever-ready cry for tolerance when sin was involved.

When unfaithful members began to realize that Brother Kramer did not have the support of the church conference, they began to appeal to the conference for sympathy. This brought increasing rebellion against Brother Kramer's efforts.

Brother Kramer began to see the futility of working under these conditions, even though he had the support of many members who desired what he taught as God's will and plan for His church.

The Kramers continued seeking God's will for their future. They determined to be faithful if it meant standing alone. Brother Kramer often expressed appreciation for and encouraged those who responded to his plea for holiness of life. This brought an increasing unity among the faithful.

One young sister who was working away from home recalls specifically a letter she received from Brother Kramer and his wife. The letter encouraged her to be well-rooted and grounded in the truth and not to be led astray by the laxness in the churches around her.

A Stand for Truth

She shared with Brother Kramer some of her experiences in the new location that were not as they should have been, yet she tried to impress on him how nice the people were. He reminded her that it is to God that she would give account, and that His Word would be the judge of her deeds.

"I realize I have failed," she admitted to him, "but they are all so nice, and no one made me feel condemned. They were all so kind and accepted me without making me feel guilty."

"To cause a person to feel uncondemned in wrongdoing is not a kindness," Brother Kramer warned. "It is a deception that will rob the wrongdoer of what it takes to bring him to repentance."

Brother Kramer's love and kindness were so evident that the young sister could not help but feel that the stern warning was evidence of love and concern. She awakened to the real condition of the churches that were without the discipline she had known in the home congregation. She soon moved back to her home community and the safety of a church that cared enough to discipline according to the Word of God.

6

A Bishop Without a Church

Brother Kramer continued to hold before the people the lofty standard of "holiness, without which no man shall see the Lord." He loved the Lord and had a genuine love for the souls of men. Though a kind, compassionate man, he was firm when it came to dealing with sin—even when members of his own family were involved. His zeal for the truth caused him to be admired and respected by some and despised and rejected by others.

Some of his detractors accused him of becoming increasingly ultraconservative, when in fact he was remaining true to long-standing convictions—convictions that were tested again and again in the years before his move to Virginia.

The differences between him and the other bishops in the conference became so evident by 1959 that

A Bishop Without a Church

he realized he could no longer remain a part of the Virginia Conference and be faithful to God and his ordination vows. Night and day, he remembered the charge laid upon him before God and His church: "Dear Brother, you are chosen to the office of bishop in the church of Christ. It will be your duty to preach the Word of God; . . . to excommunicate from the church . . . those who transgress the commands of Christ and continue in their disobedience; and when they repent and return to obedience, to receive them again. . . . Be a faithful shepherd of the flock of God, that at last you may also be received by the Great Shepherd of souls with: 'Well done, good and faithful servant. . . .' "

As a part of the conference body, Brother Kramer found it increasingly difficult to administrate Scripturally without causing friction with or receiving interference from the other conference bishops. This was confusing to the brotherhood and demoralizing to those desiring a Biblical life and practice.

After spending time in the Word, with prayer and fasting, Brother Kramer concluded that he had only one right option, though it could mean standing alone as a bishop. He felt confident that other faithful brethren also longed to get back to Scriptural standards of life and practice. But were they ready for something as radical as he was contemplating?

"We must withdraw from the conference," he told Mary one day after they had earnestly sought the Lord's leading. "I do not know if anyone will stand with us or not, but we will obey God. I believe others will follow, but I don't know how soon. Are you willing to take this stand with me?"

"Yes," his wife replied with tears, wondering what the outcome would be.

"We cannot help the church by staying in the conference and going along with unscriptural practices. We tried this long enough. We must try something different to save ourselves and others who have a desire for truth.

"Many people do not understand our concern. Perhaps they can see it more clearly if we do not drift along with them. I am convinced the Lord is asking us to take this step now. We must put our efforts into building the church, instead of struggling against the tide of worldliness." Firm in his decision, he immediately made plans to carry it out. "We will not try to persuade any of our members to follow us in this decision. If they do, however, we will encourage them. Each one must personally make his decision."

Sister Mary supported her husband's decision, faithfully standing with him, as she had in previous difficult decisions. They had faced many trying situations together, and God had always been faithful. Being confident of their faithful Guide's direction, they again would take a giant step of faith.

"We will go to Amelia on Sunday morning," Brother Kramer said. "We will tell the Pilgrim church about our decision. Then the following Sunday, we will make the same announcement here at Deep Creek."

On Sunday morning, November 8, 1959, it was

A Bishop Without a Church

with heavy hearts that Brother and Sister Kramer found their way to Amelia, Virginia.

Everyone at Amelia welcomed their bishop's presence and waited attentively for what he had for them that morning.

Brother Harvey Mast stepped behind the pulpit and greeted the congregation. "We are surprised but happy to have Brother and Sister Kramer with us this morning," he began. "Their presence is always welcome."

The expression on many faces in the audience accorded with Brother Harvey's statement.

"We will come before the Lord in prayer before we look to Brother Kramer to bring us what the Lord has laid on his heart today," Brother Mast said before leading the congregation to the throne of grace.

Brother Kramer brought a message, and at the close of the service, he stood silently for a moment, looking out over the congregation. He then said, "I stand before you in fear and trembling. I am sure you are aware of the struggles we have been having in the Deep Creek and Mt. Pleasant congregations. I can no longer stay with the Virginia Conference and fill my God-given responsibilities." After explaining some of his reasons for withdrawing from the conference, Brother Kramer said, "So this leaves me without a church, and you without a bishop."

Brother Kramer took his seat.

The Amelia brethren were aware of their bishop's struggle with the conference and the ongoing drift. But this was shocking! Few anticipated such a drastic move.

Most were still hoping that conditions would improve.

Before he dismissed the service, Brother Harvey invited all that had interest to come to his house to consider this matter together.

The brethren were concerned. Could they stand without Brother Kramer, a small group within the conference? Without Brother Kramer, how would they get the needed direction? "How do we go from here?" was the question on many hearts. It would take time for the brethren to realize what had just taken place and the impact it would have. What would this do to their children's faith in God and to the confidence and security they enjoyed in the church?

In that afternoon meeting of the Amelia brethren, Brother Harvey expressed concern for the evident apostasy in the church. "We want to be sure we are taking a Scriptural stand," he encouraged the church. "It is not a matter of *who* is right, but *what* is right."

The entire congregation was with Brother Harvey in his conclusion, and together they felt inclined to stand with Brother Kramer in his decision.

No one at Deep Creek expected the Kramers to return from Amelia before the first of the week. The Kramers had changed their plans because visitors from the Mt. Pleasant congregation were present at Amelia that morning, and Brother Kramer did not want word to reach the Deep Creek brethren before he could inform them himself. Surprised glances greeted the Kramers when they walked into the service at Deep Creek that Sunday evening on November 8, 1959.

A Bishop Without a Church

As he met an older sister upon entering the church, he simply said, "We changed our plans."

She replied, "A wise man will often change his mind."

Several topics by lay brethren were planned for the evening service. Brother Kramer did not interrupt the order of the service, but waited until time for closing announcements.

"Is there anything else?" the moderator asked, glancing in Brother Kramer's direction.

Brother Kramer raised his bowed head and nodded, slowly getting to his feet. He faced the congregation as they waited expectantly for their leader to speak. He made his announcement of withdrawal from the conference. Then, as he had at Amelia, he stated, "You are now a church without a bishop, and I am a bishop without a church. I am not deciding for you. Each one must decide for himself."

The service was dismissed.

A young brother in shock and bewilderment met Brother Kramer at the back of the church and asked him, "What are we to do?"

Brother Kramer replied with a pained smile, "That is something you will need to decide."

Brother Kramer steadfastly refused to pressure anyone to follow him. He only encouraged all to be true to God. He refused to discuss his plans or to speculate on the outcome of events. He was fully committed to stand alone if need be.

As at Amelia, this was a shock. Many hearts were touched and challenged as Brother Kramer took his stand. Many had felt for some time that something needed to be done, but would they agree to something this drastic?

Many grieved at the thought of leaving the congregations and the conference to which they had belonged for so long; it was unheard of. Truly, it was no light matter. Yet they had appreciated their faithful leader, and many felt that they must now stand with him for truth.

The following Monday morning, there was a stir among the members of the Deep Creek congregation. They were facing a crisis. Yet, no one could be certain who was for—and who was against—this move by Brother Kramer.

A few families, though they had supported Brother Kramer up to this time, were definitely not for a move so radical. One sister called another sister in the congregation. "Well, I guess Eli Kramer will learn now what his followers think of him!" she said. "He will be dropped like a hot potato! The very idea of carrying it this far! I suppose he expects a following—thinks he will end up being another 'famous Menno Simons.' He'll soon find out. Of course, we appreciated his stand—but to turn his back on the church is not the answer. Who does he think he is anyway? I never heard of such a thing in my lifetime. Leave the church to correct a problem! Never! We need the church. I thought he was stronger than to run away from his responsibility just because a few people don't agree with his way of working." When the other sister remained quiet, the calling sister soon hung up and decided to try someone else.

Brother Kramer had little support from the Mt. Pleasant congregation, but he had expected as much. For some time already, he had been termed an *alarmist* or *radical* in his efforts to bring about a revival in the churches. Many appreciated his preaching, but not his efforts at keeping the church pure. They wanted no one to meddle into their personal lives. That was their private affair.

Brother Kramer had not come to this decision rashly or hastily. He was fully aware that the majority would not stand with him and that he could anticipate much pressure. But he also knew there were sincere souls who would be willing to stand for truth and right.

7

FACING THE CHALLENGE

On Sunday afternoon, November 15, 1959, a number of concerned brethren from the Norfolk district met at the Beachy Amish school near Kempsville, Virginia, to discuss matters further. Paul Landis, then living at Hartville, Ohio, was present and was asked to lead the meeting.[1]

Brother Kramer was not involved in planning the meeting. He was welcomed, but he chose not to attend. He would give no direction to the members

---

[1] Paul Landis had been asked earlier to help with the church at Deep Creek, but he had decided instead to accept the request to move to Hartville because of the publishing work. He did, however, make the drive to Virginia many times to attend the meetings of the concerned brethren who left the conference, and helped guide the new church in the many decisions they faced.

Facing the Challenge

of the Virginia Conference churches. They must make their own decisions. He would not interfere.

They had a time of prayer, after which the meeting was opened for discussion. Those gathered soon discovered that not everyone present was of the same mind. One person referred to the Scripture that says, "Mark them which cause divisions and offenses." He indicated that the meeting was out of order.

Then the moderator rightly pointed out that this Scripture concludes with "contrary to the doctrine which ye have learned; and avoid them." The verse would not apply to that group, because what they were seeking was not contrary to the doctrine which they had learned and had been taught by the Scriptures.

The deacon from Mt. Pleasant, who was sympathetic, cautioned that the meeting could be viewed as rebellious, and if it proceeded, discipline could follow.

Prior to the meeting, the deacon of the Deep Creek church, who was an earnest conference supporter, had visited an interested member, Brother Paul Zook, who was the father of a large family. The deacon had solemnly warned Paul not to attend that meeting on the basis that it was heresy and a divisive spirit at work in the church. "You don't want to depart from the faith now with so many young people in your home," he reasoned. "I am sure they would all follow you. Your family has faithfully followed your example and embraced the faith. Now think of the consequences if you lead them into error.

"Then when you see your mistake and want to

65

return, do you think they will follow you back? I doubt it. Your children are in the church. Be satisfied with that and keep them there."

Paul did reconsider. *It is truly a serious matter. I thank God that my children are faithful. Am I thinking wrong?* he asked himself. *My intention is to stay with the faith of our fathers, but the conference is departing from the faith.* He spent several days weighing his decision. *I am certainly not against the new movement. Perhaps I should have more time to see how things will turn out. I know the church to which we now belong is going into apostasy, and there is little support from the conference officials to stop it.*

On Sunday afternoon, Paul finally informed his family of his decision. "I don't believe I'll go to the brethren's meeting. We will continue to seek God's will. I may decide to go to some meetings later, depending on what develops. Let's take more time to think and pray about it."

Two of the older daughters were very disappointed and asked if they could walk over to the Kramers for a visit that evening. Their parents consented.

Brother Kramer's strength of character and calm trust impressed the young sisters. "I am simply waiting on the Lord to accomplish His purpose for the good of the church," he said. "I am not discouraged or overanxious about standing alone. I believe God has others who will stand with me." His confidence in the Lord was well expressed as he quoted the words of the apostle Paul: " 'And we have confidence in the Lord touching you.' Our prayer for the church is that the Lord will

Facing the Challenge

'direct your hearts,' and we believe there will be many faithful ones."

As usual, the Kramers encouraged the young sisters to remain faithful to the Lord and to allow Him to lead in their lives. He encouraged them to submit to their parents during this time of transition. The encouragement received from their visit to the Kramers well compensated for the disappointment of their father's not attending the afternoon meeting.

Paul did not miss much by not attending. The main thing that came out of the meeting was plans for another meeting in two weeks on November 29.

On November 27, 1959, the Executive Committee of the Virginia Mennonite Conference met with the members of the Norfolk Council to discuss the matter at hand.

In this meeting there was a wide range of sentiments toward Brother Kramer and his concerns. Some were supportive and others were not. Someone expressed a concern that incorrect accusations had been circulated against Brother Kramer, which had caused friction in the Norfolk district council. One brother suggested that they not blame Brother Kramer too much. They discussed another minister from the district who contributed to the problem by refusing to attend the council and then failing to cooperate with decisions made in his absence. Another made a plea to be charitable with Brother Kramer.

At the end of the meeting, it was decided that Brother Philip Miller and Brother Charles Warfel convey to the concerned brethren of the district the willingness of the Executive Committee to meet with them for mutual discussion of concerns, suggesting that no hasty moves be made by anyone until such discussion could be held.[2]

So before the meeting of the concerned brethren scheduled for November 29, the request came from the Executive Committee proposing a meeting date of December 6, 1959. The concerned brethren then postponed the meeting scheduled for November 29.

On December 6, the meeting took place with J. Ward Shank, Ralph F. Heatwole, and Linden M. Wenger as conference representatives.[3] The meeting began as an open meeting of worship and counsel, for clarification of certain matters pertaining to administration. An opportunity was given for any questions. Afterward, opportunity was also given for anyone to meet with the visiting conference representatives privately.

Later, perhaps the same day, the concerned brethren with whom the conference representatives had met gathered for a time of comparing notes, but they concluded that the conference representatives had little to offer. The concerned brethren summarized the essence of the meeting in this way: "They asked for our loyalty, but could not assure us that there would be a change in direction."

---

[2] From minutes of the meeting of the Executive Committee of the Virginia Mennonite Conference with members of the Norfolk Council held at Mt. Pleasant Church, Nov. 27, 1959.

[3] Confirmed from an Executive Committee report dated December 12, 1959.

Facing the Challenge

On Monday evening, December 7, 1959, the concerned brethren met at the Paul Zook home to consider matters further. Sixty-four were present for the meeting. Brother and Sister Kramer were not present. Brother Roy Miller, who was not ordained, led out at the request of the brethren.

They sang, " 'Faith of our fathers! holy faith! / We will be true to thee till death!' " which aptly expressed the fervent desire of the group. After singing and prayer, Brother Roy opened the meeting with a plea for everyone to freely express his concerns and possible solutions, with due respect for the church and her leaders.

A number of brethren expressed concern for the trends evident in the district and fears that they would get worse. Some stated that they were ready to consider something else. As the meeting progressed, the conviction developed that the time had come to take a stand.

Those who were more timid were encouraged, along with the more aggressive ones, to express their concerns and to share any potential possibilities for the future. A desire to uphold fundamental, Biblical doctrines, Biblical holiness of life, and a Biblical standard of practice was the united thought.

"Brother Kramer is our God-chosen bishop," one brother stated, and the others all agreed. "He is standing for truth; why don't we stand with him? We could continue as an established church under his leadership. We will need to withdraw from the conference."

"We do not want something new, as we have been

accused of. Our only aim in starting a new church is to hold fast to time-tested Biblical principles, while others are compromising and bringing worldliness into the church," one of the brethren summarized. Many heads nodded.

"Brother Kramer has faithfully served among us, earnestly contending for the faith by word and example," said another. "Are we ready to follow his example now? Will we stand with him? It is always easier to follow the crowd and drift downstream. Will we battle upstream, still clinging to the historical, Scriptural faith of our fathers, or will we succumb to the pressures?"

After the brethren spent some time searching the Scriptures and discussing certain fundamental Bible doctrines, Brother Miller said, "We will now consider the meeting dismissed. Those who wish to consider further moves may remain.

"We will then proceed to make our decision official by informing the conference bishops of our intentions. We will no longer consider ourselves members of the Deep Creek congregation or part of the Virginia Conference."

He paused, giving time for those who were not so inclined, to leave before he continued the meeting. A small number got up and found their way out the door. (Some of those who left did unite later with the new church.)

A united group remained. Those remaining enjoyed a sense of freedom, and everyone relaxed. Children waited quietly, sitting on the floor at their

Facing the Challenge

parents' feet, while consideration was given to the mechanics of withdrawing from the conference to organize a sound, Biblical church.

They drew up a statement and placed it on the large dining-room table. The statement was similar to the one Brother Kramer had submitted to the conference bishops earlier. "This is not to push anyone into making a decision if you need more time," Brother Miller explained. "It is only intended as an effort to make our desire official."

Wives looked to husbands, and young Christians looked to parents for help in making this final decision. Was this the time to sign the official paper? It was a serious matter to all.

A reverent hush now filled the house as families clustered together, discussing the matter in undertones in the corner of the dining room, in the hallway, outside on the back steps, or wherever they found a little privacy.

After these short consultations, assured that they were ready to step out in faith, one family after another stepped up to the table. Father read the statement and signed his name. Then Mother and the children followed his example. One by one, others walked into the dining room and signed, until every member who had remained had officially withdrawn from the conference church.

The consensus of the brethren was to have Brother Kramer continue as bishop in this new church.

Upon the brethren's request, Brother and Sister Kramer now joined the meeting. Brother Kramer, their newly recognized leader, moderated the remainder of the meeting.

"Now, where do we go from here?" Brother Kramer asked. "We do not know if any other churches will fellowship with us and the Pilgrim church at Amelia, but our loyalty is to God, not to a conference. God will provide for us, and perhaps others will soon see the need of taking this step also. However that may be, we will remain true, and I believe the Lord will bless.

"Another immediate need to consider is a meetinghouse for worship. Together we must seek the Lord. We do not know how our needs will be met, but we know the Lord is faithful."

The meeting was dismissed, and everyone went home, feeling a keen awareness of his responsibility to be loyal to his commitment, with a confidence that God would continue to lead them. They had taken a stand for truth, and truth would prevail.

In December of 1959, the Pilgrim congregation at Amelia, Virginia, also officially withdrew from the conference, sending a letter of withdrawal to the Executive Committee of the conference. The letter, signed by Harvey Mast and Levi Kramer, stated that the withdrawal included forty-eight members, which was the entire congregation. In a letter of acknowledgment, dated December 14, 1959, the Executive committee stated their regret that the conference was losing the benefit of their fellowship and cooperation. The letter also expressed regret that they saw fit to withdraw from conference without an

Facing the Challenge

opportunity for consultation.[4]

Wednesday, December 9, 1959, was the first regular service for the new group of former Deep Creek members. It was fitting that it was a prayer meeting and that it was held in the home of the oldest member of the group, Ira M. Zook, age eighty-six years. Thirty-six people attended.

"We are now a church, but without a meetinghouse," one brother stated.

Brother Eli Kramer and Brother Paul Landis led in this service. They discussed their goals and the practical aspects of new beginnings, such as where they would meet. They would work out other details later.

On December 10, Brother Kramer and Brother Henry Zook met with the deacon of the Deep Creek congregation and some of the Mt. Pleasant ministry to inform them of the decision. At this meeting, the deacon requested that the Sunday school teachers come back and take their places on Sunday. "Do you realize that every one of our Sunday School teachers is in your group? We are not prepared to have Sunday school until we have time to reorganize." He further stated, "You are taking all the good ones. Don't you people realize your responsibility to stay and help us build the church? How do you think we can maintain any standard if all our members who want a standard are gone? You who have convictions

---

[4] Confirmed in copies of letters from the Archives of the Virginia Conference at EMU.

ought to stay with us and do your part. We need your witness."

This troubled Brother Henry. He had been a loyal church member. Had he made a mistake? After consideration and prayer, he again concluded that his loyalty was to God and His Word, not to a conference that was departing from the truth. With a regained confidence that he had done right in leading his family to where they were, he was at rest.

So the discourse continued. "Yes," Brother Henry agreed meekly, "but we have found that you don't want what we believe to be truth. Why would you want us back teaching?"

"What do you think you are gaining by isolating yourselves?" the deacon now challenged in return. "If you think you won't have any problems, you will soon find out that you aren't all perfect either."

"We realize that. We were only asking that, when there are problems, they will be dealt with in a Scriptural way, as Brother Kramer has tried to do," Brother Henry responded in all sincerity. "We cannot feel confident that this will happen in the conference by the bishops who have accused Brother Kramer of being divisive and mutilating the church. So, recognizing that we are not all perfect, we want the Scriptural safeguard of a church with a standard and a discipline that is lived out as well as taught."

"Aren't you concerned enough about the rest of us to stay and help us?"

Facing the Challenge

"We've tried that for years, and it hasn't worked. Perhaps we can help more effectively by taking a stand for truth, even if it means separating ourselves."

Here the conversation ended, and the deacon left.

8

KEEPING THE FAITH

Those first days brought much rejoicing and hope. Soon, however, the new congregation was called upon to go through experiences that tried their souls.

Testing from without was expected. What was not expected was the testing that came from within. The new church discovered that it was not enough to be *against* something. The true basis for unity is found in the truth. All agreed that the conference was taking them in the wrong direction. When the leaving-conference detail was taken care of, they found—to their dismay—that they were not agreed on where they were going nor on how they were going to get there.

Again, thank God for faithful leaders. In time, most of the brethren were brought together as to how to follow the simple teachings of the Scripture.

Keeping the Faith

Some left. Others proved untrue and needed discipline. It was a time that caused heart-searching as never before. Thank God for His faithfulness in leading this small group of believers by the hand.

Brother Kramer stated that he had not left the conference because of problems coming into the church, but because of the lack of willingness to do anything about them. Some of his own experiences with false accusations brought that out. Even though other leaders had known of these problems, nothing was done to correct them. The problems the conference bishops were currently facing made a formidable list: immodesty in attire, the unequal yoke in business, women cutting their hair and discarding their coverings, lack of loyalty and respect, use of tobacco and television, and failure to respond to teaching.[1]

His experiences while with the Ohio Conference gave Brother Kramer insight and courage in what he was now facing. He clearly saw that Virginia Conference churches were rapidly moving in the same direction the Ohio Conference had taken. Only by a firm commitment to God's requirements and a willingness to discipline and correct the problems that existed could the new church survive as a pure and godly congregation.

Some, no doubt, took refuge in the fact that the Norfolk district was more conservative than most other districts in the Virginia Conference. Not Brother

---

[1] As conference minutes verify, the bishops admitted that these problems existed, and yet they failed to take the action required to correct the problems.

Kramer! Time was to prove him right.

Sister Catherine Zook observed, "They say that Brother Kramer would not cooperate. I say Brother Kramer would not compromise."

The brethren faced decisions. They encountered many rebuffs. Many prayers ascended—prayers for wisdom, prayers for courage, prayers in behalf of those who faced encounters from members from their former settings, prayers for broken family ties.

While most families came unitedly, some did not. These often faced severe tests.

One such incident occurred soon after the beginning of the new group. A relative approached a family who had taken the step out of the conference. "You don't want to do this," she said with great agitation. "Please," she pleaded, "think what you are doing. You can leave the church, and in a few years, when you realize your error, you can return and repent, but think of Grandpa—he has been a faithful church member all his life. He followed you because most of his children and grandchildren did. He is not going to live much longer. Then think how you will feel when you are all safely back in the church and he died outside the church and won't have opportunity to repent."

Neither Grandpa nor his children were greatly disturbed by this outburst, because Grandpa was in a Scriptural church and was prepared to meet the Lord.

The Norview church building, presently unused, had served as a mission outreach facility by the conference church. Brother Kramer now asked permission

Keeping the Faith

of the Virginia Conference church to use the Norview building for services.[2] The conference granted permission for a limited time. The first Sunday morning service at the mission church building at Norview was December 20, 1959. Most of the former Deep Creek Sunday school teachers were reappointed to continue with the classes they had had in the conference church. To save the thirty-six-mile, round-trip drive to Norview, midweek prayer meetings were in the homes of members in the Deep Creek community. The Norview building served for Sunday morning preaching services only.

At the first Sunday morning service in the Norview building, ninety-six were present. This included a number of community people who had attended the mission before. The members, along with the visitors, enjoyed hearing Brother Kramer preach again, as with freedom he unburdened his heart, unhindered by the shackles that had so recently bound him.

After the message, Brother Kramer made a few comments about a church in Canada who had asked for his help to become established in sound doctrine and practice apart from their conference setting.

He also discussed a need for a statement of standards, saying, "Until we formulate our own, we will use the same statement that is being used in the conference. The ministry have the authority and responsibility to see that it is preached and practiced."

---

[2] The mission work at Norview had been closed down when Paul Landis moved to Hartville, Ohio, in July of 1959.

79

With Christmas drawing near, someone reported that the conference church did not intend to continue their long-standing practice of caroling that year due to the small number left at the Deep Creek congregation. The new church decided that they would carry on the practice, since many families in the community looked forward to this annual singing in their homes. In the conference, only the youth participated. Since the youth group in the new church was small, the parents and younger children were encouraged to join them. In an attempt to keep the lines of fellowship clear between the two groups, they did not invite conference members to participate in any worship services or mission activities.

On December 25, the new church enjoyed an evening service in the Kramers' home. They spent the evening singing and testifying.

The Sunday morning services continued in the Norview building through the month of January.

In the Oak Grove community, a small, unused schoolhouse became available. The church soon rented the building and began meeting there on February 7, 1960. This location was only about eight miles from Deep Creek, and everyone was glad to make the change to a closer location.

9

THE NEW CHURCH

"What is the name of your new church?" was a question frequently asked of the members of the new congregation.

"Kramerites" was a term attached by some outside the congregation.

"We are still Mennonites. We continue to keep the Scriptural doctrines as we always have," Brother Kramer meekly replied when approached in this way.

"Perhaps we should give our congregation a name before some of these other titles stick," he suggested to the group.

At the next meeting there was opportunity for anyone to give suggestions.

They considered many suggestions, including using the same name as the Pilgrim congregation in Amelia, since the two churches were in fellowship.

However, for the sake of differentiating between the two, it seemed more appropriate for the congregations to have different names.

Brother Landis suggested choosing a meaningful name. The brethren considered many meaningful suggestions—some to location, others to purpose. Hope Mennonite Church was the name chosen.

"We have a sure hope, anchored in God, and we want to keep that hope before us as our goal as we continue seeking the Lord in building and maintaining a pure church," Brother Landis said with confidence and assurance. Everyone readily accepted this name, a reminder of a sure hope in Christ.

"It is very fitting," Brother Kramer agreed. "It will be a constant reminder to keep that hope in view and not to allow our attention to be drawn to the things of this life."

Brethren found it more comfortable to say "I am a member of the Hope Mennonite Church" than "I am a member of the nonconference group" or "I am a member of the new church."

All Sunday and midweek services were now at the Oak Grove schoolhouse. The congregation was becoming too large for the homes to accommodate any regular meetings.

A sisters' "service circle" was organized with the intent of meeting needs within the local fellowship, in the neighborhood, and abroad. Service opportunities other than sewing were considerations, hence the name service circle.

The New Church

Many decisions now faced the Hope church. A building fund was started in hopes of soon having a meetinghouse of their own.

April 17, 1960, was a memorable day for the Hope church as they observed their first Communion since the church began. Brother Kramer brought the message and served Communion. In the afternoon they held several cottage meetings (short, in-home services) in the community and delivered several fruit baskets to poor or sick people. In the evening they enjoyed a hymn sing.

Mervin Bear, Elmer Grove, and Arnold Witmer, brethren who were in sympathy with Hope, brought a series of messages on the weekend of June 8–12, 1960. The preaching drew the Hope church together in love and unity. Each member sensed his personal responsibility in the ongoing work of the church as he listened to the inspiring messages.

The Hope church at Deep Creek continued to prosper. Since they did not deem it wise to continue sending their children to the school operated by the conference church, they started their own school in the fall of 1960. This left the conference church with only five students, whom they decided to send to public school. They then closed their parochial school.

The Hope church asked to rent the conference school building, since it was conveniently located in the middle of the Deep Creek community. The thirteen school children from Hope would all have been able to walk to school.

The Deep Creek congregation agreed to this

arrangement, but in August they decided not to rent the building to Hope after all. Undaunted, the Hope church immediately made plans to build a school. Using building-fund monies, work on the new building began immediately. It would be a small, one-room block building with a concrete floor. The Lord graciously provided, the work was completed, and the school opened on October 11, 1960.

In spite of the late notice, Sister Ruth Miller consented to be the first teacher.

In the late '50s and early '60s, an awakening swept through many more churches across the country. These people called for help to leave apostate conferences or congregations. As the revival spread, concerned leaders recognized the need for sound, Biblical literature. The Mennonite Publishing House was no longer producing satisfactory materials. The need for a new publishing work was an increasing burden of the revival leaders.

The leaders had a number of meetings to chart the course for a new publishing work. Under their direction, Brother Paul Landis, having special interest in publishing, moved to Ohio in July, 1959, to assist in a Biblical publishing work. Later he moved to Kentucky to continue the work that is now called Rod and Staff Publishers.

10

THE BLESSINGS OF A TRUE FELLOWSHIP

Now that the Hope church had their own school building and kept it heated all winter, the building could, without added expense, also serve for church services. This would save the cost of rent for the Oak Grove meetinghouse as well. So each weekend they pushed the school desks against the walls and set up folding chairs.

The faithful janitor, Mose Jarvis, an elderly black gentleman who enjoyed attending the Oak Grove services, was quite disappointed when he learned of the plans to discontinue services there, though he was not interested in becoming a member.

Since Brother Kramer believed strongly in a plural ministry, he suggested ordaining one from among the brethren in the Hope congregation. The counsel to proceed with ordination was clear, and the ordination was scheduled for January of the new year.

Since the minister ordination was planned for January 1, 1961, the Oak Grove meetinghouse was retained until after that, in expectation that the gathering would be too large for the small schoolhouse.

Brother Kramer asked Brother Roy Geigley from Pennsylvania, who had also withdrawn from the conference, to help with the ordination. Brother Roy brought a preparatory message on December 30, 1960. At that service, the members of Hope gave their nominations. Brother Henry Zook and his son-in-law, Brother Marion Miller, were nominated.

Sunday evening, January 1, 1961, one hundred ninety people crowded into the Oak Grove meetinghouse for the ordination service. Filled with a spirit of awe and reverence, the worshipers waited prayerfully and expectantly. Brother Kramer and Brother Geigley felt the weight of responsibility in this church work as they took their places on the platform. The lot was used to discern which of the two God would choose. Brother Marion Miller drew the lot.

The congregation accepted this choice as from God and worked together with their young minister.

Following this ordination, Brother Kramer began spending more time with the Amelia congregation. He also made many trips to various other churches across the States and Canada as they called for his help in finding their way out of apostate settings.

In his zeal to contend for the faith, Brother Kramer

The Blessings of a True Fellowship

was often accused of being divisive. However, his aim was to work toward true unity based on Gospel obedience, which naturally divided between those seeking to be Scriptural and those going into apostasy.

The Deep Creek conference church became quite concerned when the Hope church began regular services in their new school building just a mile down the road. "You will give us problems," they worried. "Neighbors are wondering what happened to the Mennonites. Why can't they worship together? Why two churches in one small community?"

In 1960, four members in the conference church at Crockett, Kentucky, chose to be a part of the nonconference-church movement. Since Brother Paul Landis had spent some time serving in this church earlier, they sought his help now again. They asked Brother Kramer to serve as bishop. When Brother Paul moved from Hartville, Ohio, back to Kentucky, a nonconference church was organized. The members enjoyed rich spiritual blessings under Brother Kramer and Brother Landis's leadership. Sound convictions and applications were established. With Brother Paul's family and a new convert from the community, the church soon had nine members.

The new publishing work in which Brother Paul Landis was involved now moved from Hartville, Ohio, to Crockett, Kentucky. Brother Kramer encouraged his churches to support this work by writing sound doctrinal articles and stories for publication for the encouragement of the revival churches and any others seeking for truth.

Earnestly Contend for the Faith

When members from the congregations that Brother Kramer shepherded were asked to move to Kentucky to help in the work, he encouraged them to go. One young sister, after moving to Kentucky for this purpose, enjoyed the work and decided to stay, so she requested a transfer of her membership. When Brother Kramer sent her church letter, he also sent a personal letter showing his interest in the members at home or away.

> *Dear Sister,*
> *We are happy that you enjoy the work and want to place your membership where you are living. It is best, if one is away from the home congregation, to place his membership where he is now residing. I think you have a wonderful opportunity to be used of the Lord in a good environment. Things are uncertain in the world and in the church, that is, from a human standpoint. All things are clear to the Lord, and His Word and promises are sure. Keep looking up, for your redemption draweth nigh.*
>
> *Eli and Mary Kramer*

The Blessings of a True Fellowship

Brother Kramer's approval gave her the same feeling of security and well-being under the leadership at Crockett that she had known under his leadership.

In less than two years from the time of his withdrawal from the conference, Brother Kramer had charge of three growing churches—the Hope church in southeastern Virginia; the Pilgrim church in Amelia, Virginia; and the Faith Hills church in Crockett, Kentucky. He also had the blessed privilege of seeing other churches in Pennsylvania, Ohio, Indiana, Ontario, and elsewhere returning to a Biblical foundation.

On April 15, 1962, Leroy Hooley was ordained bishop of the Pilgrim Mennonite Church at Amelia, Virginia, relieving Brother Kramer of that responsibility.

These churches, realizing the need of fellowship and encouragement on a level broader than the local congregation, grouped with other churches of like faith and began an annual fellowship meeting. They formed what is now known as the Nationwide Fellowship, agreeing to fellowship, work together, and support one another, although they did not wish to again operate as a conference that would direct local church affairs.

At the first fellowship meeting at Nappannee, Indiana, three hundred people attended. Those present at this meeting saw a notable difference from the recent conference sessions they had attended. When a faithful brother spoke out boldly against dangerous trends in the church, an echo of support rang through the audience. Support came from those who were with him in his concern and from those who were glad for the alert to the need. Unsound doctrine was immediately challenged in an effort to come to Scriptural conclusions. It was refreshing and heart-warming!

In the early 1960s, the Hope Mennonite Church began discussing the possibility of colonizing. The members felt it might be good for the church to be farther from the conference churches, with the added benefit of a witness in a new community.

Also in the early 1960s, some churches seriously considered colonizing in Central and South America. The Hope church considered such a move. However, they did not pursue it because the group was minded to remain together, and because some of the families were poor and could not see their way clear for such a move.

Several brethren began looking into the possibilities in North Carolina. They found a large tract of good farmland with which most of the group was well pleased. Those wishing to start farm operations bought most of the land and sold small lots to those wanting only a few acres.

During 1965, the families began one by one to move to Pantego, North Carolina. They worshiped in the small schoolhouse that had been erected on a lot on Main Stem Road in the Grassy Ridge community.

11

CONTENDING FOR THE FAITH TO THE END

While the Hope church was still at Deep Creek, Brother Kramer shared with his brethren that he felt that he and Mary should move to Amelia, Virginia, because of problems at Pilgrim. The Hope congregation was reluctant, but they gave him a release under the conditions. On March 11, 1964, Brother Eli and Sister Mary Kramer moved to Amelia.

At the time of the move, it was known that the Kramers wanted to be near one of their family, but it was not known that Eli's health was failing. A year after the move, it was confirmed that Eli had cancer.

Brother Kramer realized that his days were numbered, but he continued serving the Lord for the time that God had allotted him. After situating near his daughter, the Milan Hochstetler family, Brother Kramer continued to give direction to the churches under his leadership,* though he was no longer able to travel as much.

At a fellowship meeting in Ontario on August 22, 1965, one of the last that Brother Kramer was able to attend, he brought a message entitled "Gospel Holiness." His manner of preaching the Word when the message burned in his own heart inspired many to a closer walk with God. Brother Kramer made no apologies in his messages. Holy means holy—nothing more and nothing less.

A statement Brother Kramer often made was: "You can't be more holy than holy." Simple obedience and purity in every area of life is holiness, and you cannot improve on that by any amount of effort or energy. Nor can anything less than holiness meet the demands of a holy God.

On occasion, Brother Kramer was so full of the message that God had laid on his heart and so eager to share it that he began to preach enthusiastically on his way to the pulpit. This enthusiasm continued, and even gained in fervor and zeal as the message progressed. Nor did it slacken until he suddenly looked at the clock, and noticing it was closing time, closed his Bible, and stepped off the platform. A few words of encouragement while yet on the way to his seat were not unusual for Brother Kramer.

---

* Leroy Hooley had moved to Pennsylvania, and the bishop responsibility for the Pilgrim church reverted to Brother Kramer.

Contending for the Faith to the End

On September 4, 1965, the Hope congregation in Pantego rejoiced to have Brother and Sister Kramer with them for the day. Unknown to them at the time, it would be his last visit to their community. His text that morning was John 3:1–21. The message entitled "The New Birth," was clear enough for the youngest members to understand and profound enough to hold the interest and attention of the most learned. The faithful message bearer vividly portrayed the love of God.

Brother Kramer's personal interest in each member is shown in the following letter written to a young sister, in answer to a letter she had written to Brother and Sister Kramer after she experienced the new birth.

Dear Sister,

Greetings in Jesus' Name. "Whereby are given unto us exceeding great and precious promises: that by these ye might be partakers of the divine nature, having escaped the corruption that is in the world through lust" (2 Peter 1:4).

We had your welcome letter and are glad to hear of your commitment. To know that one's sins are blotted out and remembered against us no more forever makes one bubble over with joy. Read 2 Peter 1, and notice verse 10: "Wherefore the rather, brethren, give diligence to make your calling and election sure: for if ye do these things, ye shall never fall." What things? Verses 5 to 7.

Your age is the most difficult for the next few years

as you mature physically and spiritually, and you must be especially diligent or the enemy will take advantage of your immaturity.

Read Romans 12:1, 2 and then read the following verses to see how you can serve Jesus. Do all your duties heartily as to the Lord. He will reward you. Read the Scriptures for comfort when you have trials. Pray daily and never be afraid to speak for Christ.

I am feeling better, for which we praise the Lord. Pray for us.

In Christian love,
Eli and Mary

Brother Kramer, suffering increasingly from his cancer, prepared an outline for his funeral message. He finally gave up preaching from the pulpit, but many still heard powerful sermons from his bedside. Those who had come to know this spiritual giant still sought and cherished his advice and encouragement.

Sister Mary did all she could to bring relief to the sufferer, but his pain was extreme at times. He was hardly able to eat anymore, and his strength was failing fast. The days were dreary and the nights long. Yet his courage did not fail, and his zeal to build the church remained strong.

"Mother," Brother Kramer called weakly one day, "my time has come. I am no longer asking the Lord to heal my body. I will soon go to be with the Lord."

Tears came to her eyes as she tenderly smoothed the pillow and waited bravely for him to say more.

"Don't grieve, Mary," he said tenderly. "I am ready

to go. I will be glad for relief. The Lord has given us many rich blessings to enjoy together, but now He is calling me home. Are you willing, Mary? Can you say, 'Thy will be done'?"

This time Eli waited for her answer, always concerned that his loved ones submitted to God's perfect will.

Mary nodded slowly. "Yes, Eli, I want only His will. But I will continue to ask the Lord for healing if it is His will."

"No, Mother, don't," Eli groaned. "Ask Him to take me home soon," he continued, scarcely above a whisper.

"Oh, Eli, I can't."

"I wish you would, Mary. Will you?" Eli closed his eyes wearily. Mary sat by his bed a long while, thinking, searching her heart, and committing Eli to God. Her desire was still for healing if it could possibly be His will.

The years had slipped swiftly by—good years, years of joys and sorrows. God had faithfully guided and supplied their needs. How could she go on without Eli? He was so much a part of her. He had been so considerate, so wise in leading his family and the church. He had been so strong.

"Mary." His voice was very weak now as it broke into her reverie. "Have you asked the Lord to take me home soon?"

"Oh, please, Eli, I can't, not that way. I will say, 'Thy will be done,' but I want to ask for healing. He could do it yet," she pleaded.

"No, don't ask for healing—not anymore. We asked for that earlier. Now my time has come to go. I am ready. Please ask the Lord to grant me relief soon, if that is His will."

Mary meekly submitted. After a while, Eli slept.

The children were called home that night. Mary stayed near his bedside in case Eli would need her.

"It is almost unbearable to see Father suffer so," one of his daughters grieved. "I wish so much there was something I could do to give him some relief."

"The one thing that would give Father more relief than anything else in all the world would be the joy of knowing that all of his children are ready to meet the Lord and that they are serving Him faithfully," her sister replied sincerely and lovingly.

On October 23, 1966, Eli called out, "Mother, come over near my bed."

Quickly Mary responded.

"This is different." Eli spoke in a strange and husky voice.

Mary sensed the end was near and began quoting verses, knowing nothing would be more comforting than God's Word at this hour when God would separate body from spirit. " 'The LORD is my shepherd. . . . He leadeth me in the paths of righteousness for his name's sake.' "

Eli joined in. " 'Yea, though I walk through the valley of the shadow of death, I will fear no evil: for thou art with me; thy rod and thy staff they comfort me. Thou preparest a table before me in the presence of mine enemies: thou anointest my head with oil; my cup runneth over,' " Mary and Eli quoted together. His voice was growing weaker, but he continued through to the end in unison with his wife. " 'Surely goodness and mercy shall follow me all the days of my life: and I will dwell in the house of the LORD for ever.' "

For Mary, this is a treasured memory—the last thing she and Eli did together.

Then Eli began to preach as if the whole congregation were before him. "Help me to my feet," he begged. This of course was impossible. Then suddenly his voice dropped; he could hardly speak anymore but continued his message. The family all leaned nearer to catch his last words: "Earnestly contend for the faith."

Eli drew a deep breath and closed his eyes. He had finished his course; he had kept the faith. He had gone to his reward.

12

"HE . . . YET SPEAKETH"

Those who heard Brother Kramer preach remembered his messages for the heartfelt burden that so obviously lay on his heart. He preached the following sermon at a meeting in a brother's woodworking shop in Gettysburg, Pennsylvania, in July of 1960.

The Lordship of Christ
It will be a pleasure to exalt our Lord Jesus Christ here tonight. In a meeting like this, we can talk about separation and unity and about standards and many things. With all the other needs, let's not forget to exalt our Lord Jesus Christ in a special way. We have this opportunity to talk about our Lord and Saviour, and I am happy for that. I am very conscious that we will need the discussion of the brethren after this message, to bring out the things I fail to mention.

"He . . . Yet Speaketh"

I believe it is the concern of every true minister of the Gospel that his people might know the Lord. Most of our problems would be solved if every member really knew the Lord and had an intimate relationship with Jesus Christ our Saviour, the one who paid the supreme price for our redemption. If we knew Him, there would be rejoicing in our hearts; we wouldn't have time or desire to quibble about our problems.

What has happened today is that we have gone away from our Lord and have drifted into the apostasy that the Scriptures speak of as perilous times in the last days—days when the knowledge of our Lord Jesus Christ will be less and less.

I appreciate the apostle Paul, who said, "That I may know him, and the power of his resurrection, and the fellowship of his sufferings, being made conformable unto his death." He counted the things in which he could have boasted, as refuse, that he might win Him—like the young man seeks to win his lady-friend. That I might win Him—might know Him and have an intimate relationship with Him! His desire was to know the Lord and to walk with Him.

The apostle really loved the Lord, and I trust that there are many people here tonight with that kind of love for the Lord in their hearts.

Let's look at several of Paul's prayers, in which he expressed this concern. Ephesians 1— "Wherefore I also, after I heard of your faith in the Lord Jesus, and love unto all the saints, cease not to give thanks for you, making mention of you in my prayers."

Why does he mention them in his prayers? "That

the God of our Lord Jesus Christ, the Father of glory, may give unto you the spirit of wisdom and revelation in the knowledge of him."

It would be the desire of our hearts that the Lord might give unto us the spirit of wisdom and revelation—a knowledge of Him. "The eyes of your understanding being enlightened; that ye may know what is the hope of his calling, and what the riches of the glory of his inheritance in the saints."

If we could just look beyond, like Jesus did. "Who for the joy that was set before him endured the cross." Now I believe if we would just look beyond, we would not even care for one minute what the devil does against us. It would not matter if we are persecuted. That made no difference to Jesus. Because of the joy that was before Him, He endured the cross. He did not shrink from the cross for any reason. He was human like we are, yet He was divine. He can be touched with the feeling of our infirmities. He was tempted in all points like as we are, yet without sin.

If anyone ever had reason to believe that he was falsely accused, Jesus would have. Jesus didn't worry about those things at all. He came to do the Father's will, and He carried it out to the end. "He came unto His own, and His own received Him not." He loved His own unto the end. He loved until He died, and He said, "Father, forgive them; for they know not what they do." That was the attitude of our Lord Jesus Christ.

Paul expresses a desire that people might have a knowledge of Him, that they might be able to comprehend.

"He . . . Yet Speaketh"

Now let's notice another of Paul's prayers in the third chapter. "Wherefore I desire that ye faint not at my tribulations for you, which is your glory. For this cause I bow my knees unto the Father of our Lord Jesus Christ, of whom the whole family in heaven and earth is named." That includes all people, whether Christian or not—the whole family in heaven and in earth. "That he would grant you, according to the riches of his glory, to be strengthened with might by his Spirit in the inner man."

What is he praying for? "That he would grant you, according to the riches of his glory, to be strengthened with might by his Spirit in the inner man; that Christ may dwell in your hearts by faith; that ye, being rooted and grounded in love." How beautiful! And that ye may be *able*, because of this. And I tell you, my dear people, until we are rooted and grounded in the love of Jesus Christ, we cannot even comprehend the things that He has provided for the saints. "May be able to comprehend with all saints what is the breadth, and length, and depth, and height."

Ephesians 3:19. "And to know the love of Christ, which passeth knowledge, that ye might be filled with all the fulness of God."

I just wanted to share that much encouragement. "To know the Lord," I believe, is a primary concern of the Christian. By faith to know the Lord. That I may know Him, that I might have a very intimate relationship with Him, that I might know how to love and serve and please Him!

Why wouldn't I want to please Him? There is

every reason in the world why I should want to please my Lord. Why should I ever turn against Him and want my own way? Why disobey my Lord? Why would I walk away from the truth? Why should I turn away from that which He has taught me? Why should I turn my back on His Word when I love the Lord?

When we know the Lord as we ought to know Him, that makes all the difference in the world. We will immediately reach out for the things that He would teach us, and He would guide us in holiness and righteousness.

I would like to call attention to what Paul talks about in the first chapter. "Blessed be the God and Father of our Lord Jesus Christ, who hath blessed us with all spiritual blessings in heavenly places in Christ: according as he hath chosen us in him before the foundation of the world, that we should be holy and without blame before him in love."

Listen, my dearly beloved, "that we should be holy and without blame." I tell you, that is a high standard. I fear for anyone who would lower that standard. Any little compromise from the truth is not holiness.

"Having predestinated us unto the adoption of children by Jesus Christ to himself." Now, notice those beautiful words! "Having predestinated us unto the adoption of children by Jesus Christ to himself, according to the good pleasure of his will."

Notice again, "To the praise of the glory of his grace, wherein he hath made us accepted in the beloved."

"He . . . Yet Speaketh"

God has made you and me accepted in the beloved. God has accepted you and me in Him. What a wonderful position we hold in Christ Jesus!

"In whom we have redemption through his blood, the forgiveness of sins, according to the riches of his grace." You see, there we have the Lord Jesus Christ mentioned so often, just repeated over and over. I wonder how often the Lord Jesus Christ has been repeated in this series of meetings up until now. We must have Him central in our work, my dear people. I am alarmed how little we really mention Him, how small a place He has in our thinking.

You don't always have to say the name of the Lord Jesus Christ to be preaching Christ. When we preach His Word, although we don't mention His name, we have preached Christ.

In the sixth verse of the second chapter: "And hath raised us up together, and made us sit together in heavenly places in Christ Jesus: that in the ages to come he might shew the exceeding riches of his grace in his kindness toward us through Christ Jesus."

Verse 13: "But now in Christ Jesus ye who sometimes were far off are made nigh by the blood of Christ. For he is our peace, who hath made both one, and hath broken down the middle wall of partition between us." That is beautiful also. How can we break down the middle wall of partition between people?

The faith of the Lord Jesus Christ will bring people together in unity. When there is no unity, sin has entered, and it is not those who are holding to the faith of Jesus Christ who have broken that unity! It is those who have allowed sin, and brought sin into the body, who bring division. There is no unity there. Sin is a cancer, killing the body. The only possible thing to do is to put the cancer out of the body so the body can work together in unity. You put sin out, and unity immediately comes in. Let Jesus be Lord. Let the faith of Jesus Christ be first. Let it be "all in all" to every believer, and I tell you, my dear people, there is true unity of the Scriptures. The true faith will bring us together.

He has broken down the wall of partition. That has reference to the Jew and the Gentile. It is broken down between any race, or between enemies. And, friends, if anything has come between us, it is broken down. The love of Jesus Christ will do that.

"Now therefore ye are no more strangers and foreigners, but fellowcitizens with the saints, and of the household of God; and are built upon the foundation of the apostles and prophets, Jesus Christ himself being the chief corner stone."

Some of those beautiful things that Paul speaks about really thrill my soul! "That the Gentiles should be fellowheirs, and of the same body, and partakers of his promise in Christ by the gospel."

"In whom we have boldness and access with confidence by the faith of him." Now, dear people, I have boldness and confidence tonight. I have no fear of anything but sin. I am not afraid of anything that happens when I know the Lord and follow Him. And no one else needs to fear anything in any nation, kindred, people, or tongue. I don't believe people need to be scared about the devil, or anything else, when they know the Lord and are in His will.

Jesus is called the LORD Jesus Christ over and over in the Scriptures. First, in the Great Commission. "Go ye therefore, and teach all nations, baptizing them in the name of the Father, and of the Son, and of the Holy Ghost: teaching them to observe all things whatsoever I have commanded you: and, lo, I am with you alway, even unto the end of the world. Amen." And He says, "All power is given unto me in heaven and in earth." All power to Jesus. Do you have any power? Not that is worth anything. If you have any power that amounts to anything at all, it is the power of the Lord Jesus Christ. Outside of His power, you are as weak as a feather that blows in the air.

"All power is given unto me in heaven and in earth." He is Lord of heaven and earth. He is Lord and has the preeminence in all things. He is Lord, and we might as well face it. We can ignore it if we want to. The nations can ignore it. The sinner can ignore it. But in the end, Jesus Christ is Lord.

Jesus is Lord of the church, no matter what we do, no matter how we run the church, or how we administrate. Finally, Jesus is Lord of the church. If we are a part of His church, He is Lord of our lives.

The only right thing to do is to stick to His Word, regardless of what anyone else does or says. Now listen to me! It is not my interpretation; it is not what other churches say. It is *what the Scriptures say* that counts.

So let's not try to fit the Scriptures to what we

think until we have lost the faith.

Someone who has now gone to be with the Lord plainly said, "The time has come that it is necessary to make a mass movement and trim the church of bad material, if we want to save the church." That thing has been neglected. If the warning had been heeded back then, and if they would have trimmed the church of bad material, we wouldn't find ourselves where we are today, as the apostasy has swept over the church. I am not talking only about the Mennonite church, but all of Protestantism, Ecclesiasticism. Professed Christendom is in an apostate condition. We know it! Our leaders know it! Our bishops know it! I am not saying that every person in the churches is apostate. But we are all affected by it. Unless we protest, our children and grandchildren will be greatly affected by it. Unless we plead, unless we fast and pray, we will be affected more and more by it—our hearts and our practices will be affected.

"Wherefore God also hath highly exalted him, and given him a name which is above every name: that at the name of Jesus every knee should bow, of things in heaven, and things in earth, and things under the earth."

We all will do that some day. We are going to have to face it. We will bow to Him and confess that He is Lord and has a right to whatever He will do concerning our lives here upon the earth.

Jesus is Head of the nations of the world. He Himself will call for a restitution of all things. He Himself will open the seven-seal book, out of which the seven-seal judgments will come, and the seven trumpet judgments, and the seven vial judgments. These judgments will be poured out upon the earth in rapid succession. Jesus is the one who will do it, and He has the right to because *He is Lord* over all people of the earth.

Jesus Christ is in the midst of His church, as Jesus Christ is in the midst of the seven golden candlesticks in Revelation 1 and 2—not just in one particular little group, but in the midst of *His* church.

The seven golden candlesticks represent the church, and Jesus Christ is in the midst of it, and He has the right to rule. He is Lord over them, even though they do not obey Him, even though they do not walk in truth, even though they have Jezebelism or Balaamism and a lot of other isms. They have left their first love, and some have gone farther than that; they are neither hot nor cold. They say they are rich and increased with goods and have need of nothing, and they know not that they are poor and blind and naked.

Jesus says, "I will spue thee out of my mouth."

Concerning the church that does not have a love for the truth, He says, "God shall send them strong delusion." The antichrist will come and deceive them. To whom will He send a strong delusion? Not the world: they always were lost in sin. He will send the strong delusion to the apostate church so that they will believe a lie: "That they all might be damned who believed not the truth, but had pleasure in unrighteousness." That is a fearful thing, my dear people! Let us know the Lord!

Christ is Lord of all the earth. He is Lord of the church. He is Lord of His bride, the faithful church. He is Lord also of the apostates—though they are not recognizing Him as Lord now, they will bow to Him one day. He is Lord of all the nations of the world. When the time comes, He will prove to the world who is Lord and who is in control.

People do not like the idea of obedience to rules and regulations. Oh, that would be legalism. Listen to me! The Bible says, "In flaming fire taking vengeance on them that know not God, and that obey not the gospel of our Lord Jesus Christ." He says there is wrath coming on the children of disobedience.

I am sure that there are many legalistic people, living under the law of the church, who will join a group that has stepped out of the conference seeking a true fellowship. There may be those who have never been born again, who are only legalistic, who will join the true group only because the group is holding a standard.

My dear people, if there is anyone who believes in Biblical conservatism, I do! But I do not believe in asceticism. I do not believe in this attitude of wanting to do this to be more holy, and do that to be more holy, and sacrifice something else to be more holy. We are not made holy that way! Holy people are those who obey the Lord! Holy people obey the principles that are taught in the Scriptures.

Many people who don't want legalism, laws, and rules are not even obeying the plain teachings of Jesus

Christ. They do not only reject the application that the church has made to Bible principles, but they also reject the plain "Thus saith the Lord." Moreover, we as their leaders are doing nothing about it, which on our part is also rejecting the plain teachings of Jesus. We are not setting the pattern of obedience to our Lord.

The devil's lie number one started back in Eden: "Ye shall not surely die." You belong to the Lord; no, you won't die. Just a little sin—that is the eternal security doctrine. The devil is still deceiving the world: You are a Christian; you were once saved. Don't we all sin just a little? "Ye shall not surely die!"

The Bible tells us plainly what will happen if we sin. It is the fundamentalists and evangelicals of our day who are teaching this lie. It isn't the modernist or those who don't believe in God in the first place. It is the fundamentalists who are deceiving the church.

One minister said, "Since there is no way anymore that we can cleanse the church of sin, the only alternative is to accept the eternal security doctrine. It has gone too far; sin has been in the church too long; there is nothing we can do anymore." Nearly all fundamentalists of our day are accepting this devil's lie number one. Many publishers are publishing it.

How important is it to obey Christ? His teachings? His church? How important was it in the Old Testament? For one violation of the Law of God, they died without mercy.

But many say, "But we are living in a better time. Jesus saved us. God does not see our sin through the blood of Jesus." The Bible tells us, "The wages of sin is death" and "If ye live after the flesh, ye shall die: but if ye through the Spirit do mortify the deeds of the body, ye shall live."

How important is it to obey the Lord? The Book of Hebrews tells us we have a better sacrifice—not so we can keep on sinning, but so we can have victory over sin. The Book of Hebrews also tells us that "God, who at sundry times and in divers manners spake in time past unto the fathers by the prophets, hath in these last days spoken unto us by his Son." He used to talk through His prophets: Moses, Elijah, Elisha, and Gideon. He spoke through the Old Testament patriarchs. He talked to His people. It was pretty serious when God spoke. God wanted them to listen, and if they didn't listen, they were liable to the judgments of the Law, under the *merciless* Law. For them there was no mercy, but now we live under mercy. It is not God's will that one soul should perish.

Now He says that in those days he spoke to the fathers by the prophets; but in these last days He has spoken unto us by His Son. Therefore, He says, because Jesus is speaking, "we ought to give the more earnest heed." *More* heed than we did before. That is exactly opposite of the devil's lie number one.

"For if the word spoken by angels was stedfast, and every transgression and disobedience received a just recompense of reward; how shall we escape?" If we neglect to hear Jesus our Lord, if we neglect this great salvation—saved by the blood of Jesus Christ, our sins taken away—how shall we escape if we reject it? How much more we should listen when Jesus speaks. "And Moses verily was faithful in all his house, as a servant, for a testimony of those things which were to be spoken after." It says Moses was faithful. Now listen! "But Christ as a Son over his own house; whose house are we, if we hold fast the confidence and the rejoicing of the hope firm unto the end."

"Take heed, brethren, lest there be in any of you an evil heart of unbelief, in departing from the living God." Here he suggests that we can depart from the faith. "Take heed." Beware lest you let anything slip that you have heard. He goes on: "But exhort one another daily, while it is called To day; lest any of you be hardened through the deceitfulness of sin." That suggests that we can be hardened through the deceitfulness of sin. But if we were once saved anyway, does it make a difference if we sin just a little bit? Many in the church today are being hardened in the deceitfulness of sin. There are a lot of things that don't seem as sinful as they used to. We have accepted them; we take them for granted. They no longer seem sinful—the very things that were once the abominable sins in our eyes, today are accepted in many Mennonite churches.

Are we hardened? Listen, my dear brethren. God requires of us bishops that we keep house, that we deal with those sins and abominable things that destroy the spiritual life of the church. We must deal with not only the one who has committed the act, but also all that are influenced by it. And don't tell me that no one is influenced by it. I heard of a certain church who had believed that cutting hair for women was sin according to 1 Corinthians 11. One day the bishop's daughter cut her hair, and in a few weeks, there were about a dozen women in that church who cut their hair. Weren't they born again? Couldn't they go to heaven anyway? Not according to the Bible. Sin cannot enter there.

"Let us labour therefore to enter into that rest." Labor and struggle! Don't let anything slide. We never slide up—it is always downward. We can't coast into heaven. "Labour therefore."

"Seeing then that we have a great high priest, that is passed into the heavens, Jesus the Son of God, let us hold fast our profession." Hebrews 6:1: "Let us go on unto perfection." Let's not degenerate as we have been doing, but go on to perfection.

"And we desire that every one of you do shew the same diligence to the full assurance of hope unto the end . . . who have fled for refuge to lay hold upon the hope set before us" (Hebrews 6:11, 18).

Then in the tenth chapter, let's notice a few more verses. "Let us draw near with a true heart in full assurance of faith, having our hearts sprinkled from an evil conscience, and our bodies washed with pure water. Let us hold fast the profession of our faith without wavering; (for he is faithful that promised)."

"Not forsaking the assembling of ourselves together, as the manner of some is; but exhorting one another: and so much the more, as ye see the day approaching. For if we sin wilfully after that we have received the knowledge of the truth, there remaineth

"He . . . Yet Speaketh"

no more sacrifice for sins, but a certain fearful looking for of judgment and fiery indignation, which shall devour the adversaries." Then he says, "He that despised Moses' law, died without mercy."

Now he goes on to say, "Of how much sorer punishment, suppose ye, shall he be thought worthy, who hath trodden under foot the Son of God, and hath counted the blood of the covenant, wherewith he was sanctified, an unholy thing, and hath done despite unto the Spirit of grace?" That is the teaching of the Lord Jesus. Of how much greater punishment shall he be thought worthy who sins willfully—knowingly doing wrong? That is counting the blood of the covenant an unholy thing.

Hebrews 12:18–21: "For ye are not come unto the mount that might be touched, and that burned with fire, nor unto blackness, and darkness, and tempest, and the sound of a trumpet, and the voice of words; which voice they that heard entreated that the word should not be spoken to them any more: (For they could not endure that which was commanded, And if so much as a beast touch the mountain, it shall be stoned, or thrust through with a dart: and so terrible was the sight, that Moses said, I exceedingly fear and quake)."

When God spoke back there, the earth quaked, and I believe that it is important that when Jesus speaks and when the New Testament tells us something, it is important that it thunders in our ears!

Take it as if God means it when He speaks. God's Word cannot be changed. We cannot change it no matter what the culture or people. It makes no difference: When God speaks, He means what He says!

His Word is forever settled in heaven. That is for every time, culture, and age. You cannot change His Word. Never! It thundered back then at the mount.

I remember at home when we had a fire. We didn't have running water then. My father always kept a pail filled with water. He was always prepared in case of fire. One started in the little boys' bedroom. When my little brother yelled, "Fire in the house!" one night, he said he heard my father's feet hit the floor immediately. Why? He believed it, and he was prepared. He grabbed the pail of water, and the fire was soon put out. When he heard the word, "Fire!" it thundered in his ears.

Anything the Bible says ought to thunder in our ears! Our feet ought to hit the floor right now when God speaks! It should bring action immediately!

What has happened to the churches today? Are we listening to God's Word? Are we willing to obey? Are we willing to contend for it?

"See that ye refuse not him that speaketh." See that you don't refuse the Lord Jesus, for if they escaped not who refused the prophets, how do you think you will escape from Him that "speaketh from heaven: whose voice then shook the earth, but now he hath promised, saying, Yet once more I shake not the earth only, but also heaven."

HE IS LORD! He will reign, and we will bow.

* * * * *

"He . . . Yet Speaketh"

The following article, written by Eli D. Kramer, appears as it was printed in the June 1966 issue of the Pearl of Great Price, *now called* The Christian Contender, *a monthly publication by Rod and Staff Publishers. Four months after this article was published, Brother Kramer laid down his responsibility and went to his eternal reward, leaving the work to other faithful brethren.*

Authority in the Church

In our day the ministry have little they can do but preach. The general tendency is to disregard the responsibility and the authority of the ministry. Trustees of the church hire and fire ministers. But according to the Scripture "The Holy Ghost hath made you overseers" (Acts 20:28).

Who has authority in the church? First of all, God is the final, supreme authority. The Word of God is the only true source of authority. God delegates authority to men of faith, of maturity, full of the Holy Ghost, to carry out, teach, and promote the Word of God in the church. If we deviate from that, we lose our right to any authority.

The congregation has authority only as they are united in the Word of God. Any deviation from any part of the Word denies the right of authority as a congregation. The individual also has authority—authority over Satan by the Word of God.

What is the authority of the ministry and how is it exercised? The minister is called of God and by the congregation and ordained by God according to the

Word of God. If a man's call is not of God he will not get along well. He faces defeat if he is voted for carelessly or if he is not Scripturally qualified. "Unto us is given the ministry of reconciliation"—to be done Scripturally.

The ministry must give account to God as to how they handle people and how they handle the Scriptures. They must acquaint themselves with their work (1 Timothy 4:12–16).They must give no occasion for people to despise them because they are young or for any other reason (1 Corinthians 16:11; Titus 2:15).

The minister must read the Word, teach it to the people, exhort them, give himself wholly to the Scriptures. He must be careful of his own life: "Take heed unto thyself." He is to teach the doctrine in all its purity. Every carnal mind will rebel against the doctrine in all its purity. Every carnal mind will rebel against it, sinful self will rebel against it, but the newborn Spirit from God will never rebel against the truth.

"Preach the Word, not other things (2 Timothy 4:2). Preach it straight, Preach what God says. If we preach other things we will lose all right and authority to preach and be a preacher. It is the *preachers* who should do the preaching, expounding, and dividing the Word. Men whom God has called, mature men. There are few young men who can stand up and defend with zeal the doctrine of the Word. God has not intended to delegate the preaching to lay members.

Tell them they are to obey *everything*, not just part of the Word.

The church will lose her power and blessing when

"He . . . Yet Speaketh"

she begins to deviate from the Word.

Preach to everyone "in season, out of season". "Reprove, rebuke." Who loves to do it? It is the hardest thing a preacher has to do today. He can do it as gently and kindly as he can, and they will not have this man to rule over them. Preach to your children, preach to your young people, preach to your neighbor. The preacher is responsible to correct children, but if parents will not receive correction, then the children will not. The duty of the minister and the parent is to expose this evil. When the preacher cannot do anything for their children, parents often blame the preacher for it. They become very alarmed when the preacher cannot control them. Half way religion in parents is not enough to help children.

Exhort-use persuasion against people continuing in sin. Both parents and preachers need to do this. Paul did it with all humility of mind, all subjection to the Word. Preach repentance toward God and faith toward our Lord Jesus Christ.

Do the things that promote the kingdom of God. Put away childish things, and things that have no value. Have prayer publicly and from house to house. Set your affection on things above. Do not promote entertainment for the young people.

Cease not to warn every man night and day with tears. What would happen if we would have four preachers like that in this church?

What is the duty of members?

They should honor elders doubly, with their respect and their means. Rebuke him not but entreat him as a father, and the younger men as brethren. Receive not an accusation but by two or three witnesses. Obey them; submit yourself.

Members should know their minister and understand him. Contact him and fellowship with him. Esteem him very highly in love, not "if he never makes a mistake". Ministers make mistakes. If you have something at any time against your ministers, be very careful of your attitudes. I would feel it a real favor if you would come to me.

—*Eli Kramer*

* * * * *

The following article, written by Eli D. Kramer, appears as it was printed in the July 1964 issue of the Pearl of Great Price, *now called* The Christian Contender, *published monthly by Rod and Staff Publishers. The date written is unknown, but it was printed two years and four months before Brother Kramer's deliverance from the presence of sin, fulfilling the desire of his heart!*

Togetherness

After a communion service, what is next? Where do we go from here? John 17, a beautiful chapter, expresses Jesus' desire that we all may be one as He and the Father are one. Unity of spirit and faith is implied by oneness.

John 17:11 "And now I am no more in the world, but these are in the world, and I come to thee. Holy Father, keep through thine own name those whom thou hast given me, that they may be one, as we are."

"He . . . Yet Speaketh"

There is no testimony to the world as effective as the oneness of God's people. It convinces the world more than the disunity of believers. Disunity among us is the most destructive witness. "By this shall all men know that ye are my disciples, if ye have love one to another."

We hear a great deal about unity these days. I am sure the devil believes in unity. He would do anything he could to bring unity on the wrong side, not the kind God would be pleased with. I have been approached on the matter of mutilating the body of Christ. I have also experienced quite a bit of unity, praise God.

So much is said today about togetherness, trying to get the saint and sinner together. "Love, that is the principle thing in the Christian life. Love! love! love!" -they say. But there is a Scriptural love that brings unity.

Ephesians 3:14–19, In this last part of the third chapter of Ephesians, Paul speaks of love. "I bow my knees unto the Father. . . that ye, being rooted and grounded *in love*. . ." Without the love of God, there is no unity possible. Then he goes on in the next chapter, "I therefore, the prisoner of the Lord, beseech you that ye walk worthy of the vocation wherewith ye are called, With all lowliness and meekness, with longsuffering, forbearing one another *in love*; Endeavoring to keep the unity of the Spirit in the bond of peace." "With all lowliness and meekness" (not with an exalted spirit) and much forbearance.

Love holds fast to the truth. Love does not compromise. Never! That is the kind of love the devil offers, the kind that compromises. If the love of Christ is effective in our hearts, we will obey the Word. We will then love fellow believers who also obey.

"Love your enemies." Christians never turn against people. We hate the sin, we protest against it, but we do not hate the people. We heap coals of fire on their heads. Now, that does not mean piling hot coals on their heads but it means to love them until they can not stand it. Love them so much that they finally come your way.

Discipline administered with-out the love of Christ cannot be an effective discipline. There is no discipline in my life as effective as Christ's love, His chastening love to me. Under the chastening hand of the Lord, we see the love of God. Job did not blame God for all his misfortune, but said, "Blessed be the name of the Lord."

In this same chapter here in Ephesians we have the building up of the church and gifts given to us.

Verse 15, "But speaking the truth *in love,* may grow up into him in all things, which is the head, even Christ:" Speak the truth, but speak it *in love*. We can not be together with the world or with all professing believers; but we are together with all those who have experienced salvation. Colossians 2:13 We were dead in sins, but now we are alive *together*.

Ephesians 2:6. We are raised up together and made alive in one body, like the members of our bodies are alive together. We sit together in Christ. How can we sit together unless we are agreed? Amos 3:3.

The body of Christ is knit together. Colossians 2:19.

"He . . . Yet Speaketh"

We are tied to each other in love. We just would not be following the Word if we would not love. Why do we understand Scripture differently? It is because some do not want to obey.

1 Corinthians 1:10, "that ye be perfectly joined together in the same mind and the same Judgment." Love increases instead of decreases. Every true Christian will have this experience. Whenever you meet another Christian, you will feel a oneness.

Togetherness is not without some conditions.

Ephesians 2:21, 22. We are builded together for an habitation of God. God's habitation is the Church; that is where He dwells. "We will come unto him, and we will make our abode with him." God condescends to dwell within vessels of clay.

"God hath tempered the body together." 1 Corinthians 12:24. We are to care one for another. God has tempered the body, giving more abundant honor to some than to others. We will always have weak members. More honor is given to some that there be no schism in the body. Schism is that which destroys the body. It is like cancer, working against the health and life of the body. Unless something is done, this schism will destroy the body. An effort must be put forth to get rid of it. If you had cancer, or I had cancer, we would get the most effective medicine we could find to destroy the cancer before it destroyed us. If we allow the leaven of sin to continue, the whole lump will be destroyed. Sin must be dealt with. Sometimes we are more concerned about the sinner than the sin. That is the reverse. Of course, if the person does not respond, there comes a time when he must also be dealt with. He becomes a liability to the body.

2 Corinthians 6:1. We are workers *together*. I must recognize the particular place of each one in the body of Christ. Do not feel that you have no gift; do your part. A mother may feel that she is just taking care of her family, but there is no greater work than serving your children. We are workers together so no one needs to feel higher than another. What have I done for the Lord, if anything? we should ask ourselves. When called to judgment, we will not be thinking of labors performed, but of grace extended. Let us recognize another's work. God has work for us all to do and the work is great. The work reaches out beyond our small circles. There are little groups here and there, all working in the white harvest field.

2 Corinthians 1:11; Romans 15:30. We work and strive *together* in prayer. Paul prayed for himself and asked others to pray for him. Do not forget to pray. You do not have much against a brother or sister if you pray for him. If you do have a feeling against them and get down to really pray for them, you will feel differently.

Philippians 1:27, "that ye stand fast in one spirit, with one mind striving *together* for the faith of the gospel." Striving together for the Gospel is contrary to striving for unity without the Gospel. If we all strove together for the Gospel, then we would not have to discipline in the church. In our baptismal vows, we promised God to strive for Christ and His Kingdom. If we do otherwise, we have already begun to backslide.

"He . . . Yet Speaketh"

If we have the right spirit, we will respond when corrected with the truth. One way in which I can tell whether people have the Spirit of God is the attitude they take when the truth is presented to them. Spiritual people will naturally respond to truth. If they argue against it and do not accept it, I question whether they have the Holy Spirit.

Ephesians 2:6, "And hath raised us up *together*, and made us sit *together* in heavenly places in Christ Jesus;" We are one in fellowship with Christ.

Romans 8:22, "For we know that the whole creation groaneth and travaileth in pain together until now." Do you ever groan when you see the pressure of sin and strife within the church? Then we say, "Would that the Lord would come!" We constantly feel the working of Satan. We see disunity on every hand. "Oh, Lord, how long until we are delivered from the presence of sin?"

—Eli Kramer